AF265123

HEALING *in* HOPE

This devotional is a gift.

TO:

The words in this devotional are a gift
from God written with you in mind.

FROM:

DATE:

Healing in Hope
Words of Encouragement
Healing Of Painful Emotions

by

Clare Page

Healing in Hope | Clare Page
Front Cover Design| Island Printing, Gold Coast, Australia
Printing | Island Printing, Gold Coast, Australia
Photography and Word Content | Clare Page
Editing | Clare Page
Prepress | Keith Page
Reprographics | Danny Irvine Photography
ISBN |978-0-646-73464-4

Scripture quotations used in the book are from:
New International Version – 1973, 1978, 1984, 2011.
The Passion Translation-2020. English Standard Version-2001.
Amplified Bible-2015. Amplified Classic-1954, 1958, 1962, 1964, 1965, 1987. New Living Translation-1996, 2004, 2007, 2015.
The Message-1993, 2002, 2018. King James Version-1954, 2011.

About Clare

Clare Page is an Australian and International award-winning Professional Fine Art Landscape Photographer.

Her passion for photography was kindled as a teenager when she recognised photography came easily to her. She is self-taught involving the principles of photography. Clare has received tuition to fine tune her art.

The solitude of the countryside, including rivers, mountains, and lakes is what attracts Clare. Whilst she relishes in the thrill of capturing big surf. Clare captures creation through her lens and frames it with precision reflecting the spontaneity and rhythm of nature.

Clare's work is richly organic, which originates from the depth of her soul. Photography and writing are her purpose, tools that have facilitated in healing Clare from depression. She is passionate about people, philanthropy, photography, and travel.

Her passionate purpose is to equip, educate, empower, encourage and to engage with those who are seeking direction for their lives, facilitating them in cultivating hope in going forward. And fostering relationships whilst navigating the next step into the future!

Clare currently makes her home in Gladstone, Queensland, Australia.

Visit Clare's Website | clarepagephotography.com

God guided me in writing this devotional to encourage, empower and enlighten you in going forward, in Christ.

This book is dedicated to you, as you pursue God's purpose for your life. Rise up in hope. Hope is the building block and bridge to faith. It is a confident expectation that something good is going to happen to you.

You are not forgotten, nor are you overlooked, and neither are you abandoned by God. He created you as His Masterpiece for a time such as this. He will never leave you nor forsake you.

My hope and prayer is for you to galvanise your faith and hope in God, in moving forward. There is no time like the present, unwrap the wonderful gift of today and determine to let go of what lies behind and believe in who God created you to be. A history maker, a world changer, a peace maker, for His glory.

Seize the day. Live your life to the fullest, in Christ. Forgive, release, and drop every offence and live in the freedom of the Spirit. Today and every day.

Hebrews 6:19-20 Amplified Bible
19.This hope [this confident assurance] we have as an anchor of the soul [it cannot slip and it cannot break down under whatever pressure bears upon it]—a safe and steadfast hope that enters within the veil [of the heavenly temple, that most Holy Place in which the very presence of God dwells], [Lev 16:2} 20.where Jesus has entered [in advance] as a forerunner for us, having become a High Priest forever according to the order of Melchizedek. [Ps 110.4].

REST YOUR WEARY SOUL

Let it be well with your soul. Recline yourself in a posture of faith in God. Breathe easy. Inhale deep. Exhale freely. Surrender your striving to God. You matter to Him. He created you in His image.

Walk easily, upright, and allow God to take the weight off your shoulders. Take mini breaks. Resist the demands of your flesh. Let go of the shame that has threatened you, which is the result of your hiding from society, that has been happening to you for some time. Know who and Whose you are and walk in your True Identity in Christ. You are not a mistake, as you have been lied to, and you have believed in those lies.

Don't give up in believing in miracles, no matter how long the battle has been going on. Keep on walking by faith and not by sight. Fight the good fight of faith. You are gifted, talented and have come too far to permit the devil to steal your Divine destiny and inheritance. Your past does not define your identity, or your future. Be encouraged. Be at peace.

SCRIPTURE:
Matthew 11:28-30 MSG
28-30."Are you tired? Worn out? Burned out on religion? Come to me. Get away with me and you'll recover your life. I'll show you how to take a real rest. Walk with me and work with me-watch how I do it. Learn the unforced rhythms of grace. I won't lay anything heavy or ill-fitting on you. Keep company with me and you'll learn to live freely and lightly."

CALCULATED RISKS

You can remain frozen in fear or, alternatively, you can place your trust in God and leap in faith into your God-given destiny. As a Fine Art Landscape Photographer, God called me out to the ocean recently. The surf was big. But the light was out of this world. I thanked God for keeping myself and my equipment safe as He always does.

I surveyed the waves before I secured my tripod in the sand. The calculated risk was the reflection of the sun on the wet sand. I took a step of faith and advanced towards the light.

A rogue wave came rushing at me, I cried out, "Jesus", as I knew I was in trouble, and He rescued me and my equipment. But I wouldn't have experienced that short moment of light if I'd remained 'stuck' where I started! In moving forward, I knew God had me covered. As He has you, in the palm of His hand.

Do not permit fear from immobilising you. Go forward unafraid. You have nothing to lose but everything to gain.

SCRIPTURE:
Psalm 28:7 NIV
The Lord is my strength and my shield; my heart trusts in him, and he helps me. My heart leaps for joy, and with my song I praise him.

YOU ARE NOT ALONE

Soothe your soul in the healing power of God's Word. God put on my heart to drive to this incredible destination, Wellington Point, Brisbane, Australia. It was a miraculous journey from start to finish. I left home at the twelfth hour.

Obedience to God's voice led me to a scene like I'd never experienced before. Unusually, I had the place to myself. God and me. I witnessed God in the most unique way as I knelt in the shallow water. It was a heavenly, miraculous moment. The atmosphere was soothing and serene.

My journey in life at that time had been rough and tough. God knows your heart and your desires. He is calling you to experience intimacy with Him whilst He whispers to your heart. It is important for you to respond to His still, small voice.

God wants to bless you, to protect you, to commune with you, receive and respond to His whisper to your heart and soul. Shut out the distractions and the chatter.

Be blessed. Be at peace. Be still and rest in God's presence. In your times of turbulence, trials, and tests, you are vulnerable, be rest assured, you are not alone. God is with you. He is for you. God is not angry with you. Be still your beating heart.

SCRIPTURE:
Joshua 1:5 ESV
No man shall be able to stand before you all the days of your life. Just as I was with Moses, so I will be with you. I will not leave you or forsake you.

IN THE QUIETNESS OF THE MOMENT

Choose to live in audacious faith, cultivated in hope. God can release a miracle to you, through Divine acceleration. God's desire is to deliver you from the root cause of your torment. Choose to forgive. It is freeing. Forgiveness refreshes, relinquishes, and removes the hold Satan has had on your life.

God is requiring you to surrender your heart, every shattered fragment of it, and your will to Him, to be healed. Whatever you are experiencing, the acute opposition that is prevalent, is a sign of an imminent breakthrough. Rest in God's presence. When you are at the end of yourself, God works miracles.

Surrender your fleshy desires in an attempt to accomplish anything in your strength, which will result in exhaustion. This has become a repetitive cycle. Posture yourself in His grace, and only by God's grace can your hope and life be restored.

God's desire is for you to trust Him as He unravels His mysteries to you. Be still. Become increasingly expectant, let go of negative mindsets. Be impregnated in faith, for He is the God of the impossible. Give God the little you have and watch Him multiply it. As He pours His love into you, receive Him in the quietness of the moment. Linger in His loving presence.

SCRIPTURE:
Romans 16:20 NLT
The God of peace will soon crush Satan under your feet. May the grace of our Lord Jesus be with you.

GOD'S TENDER, HEALING TOUCH

Every day, be safe, in every decision you make, may it be of God. Seek His Divine counsel. Be healthy, treat your body to good food as it is the temple of the Holy Spirit.

Be kind to others and to yourself. Love, particularly when you are rejected, love from God's love. Laugh, often, even in the darkest moments, think on good things. Train your brain to refrain from seeking revenge. Let go of the past, it has no power over your present/future, unless you give it a voice. Shut it down. With God's help, wean yourself from every addiction and old, rigid mindsets,

Release your pain to God. He is your Healer. Remain in His peace. Know deep down in your heart that God loves you. Receive His love. Turn the other cheek. Unforgiveness comes at a cost. It keeps you bound in the complexities of some relationships. Bless those who curse you and pray for those who persecute you, read Luke 6:27-36.

Come out from the shadows. Shatter the old mindsets. Stop attempting to reduce God to your thinking. You are bright, beautiful, brilliant, in His Creation. You are an original. You're God's masterpiece. Live out of the ordinary, from the extraordinary, left of centre. How? By thinking of how brilliantly God created you. Stop procrastinating. Go forward unafraid. God is with you. He is for you. Break forth into joy.

SCRIPTURE:
1 Peter 2:24 NIV
"He himself bore our sins" in his body on the cross, so that we might die to sins and live for righteousness; "by his wounds you have been healed."

STAND STRONG IN CHRIST

Stand fast. Resist the temptation to abort your dreams by speaking negatively over your future. Live above your circumstances. How, you ask? Cultivate faith, invest your time in reading God's Word, attract every good thing that God has intended for you, by being faith-filled and faithful. And be a blessing to others.

Perseverance is paramount, press into God, and occupy your Divine inheritance. God is developing character in you, He is sifting you, and yes, it is painful and unpleasant, but it is worth it. The pain associated with your past has had power over you. Choose to praise God in your time of change, even though it is painful, praise is powerful. Keep your focus on the benefits of God transforming your life, one step at a time.

Don't give up hope, particularly when circumstances look bleak. Resist distractions, they are a lure from Satan to dismantle your peace. Keep on pushing and persevering until your prayers are answered and your dreams become a reality. Be at peace. The challenges will be worth it as God is using the opposition you are experiencing to equip and empower those around you who are stuck.

SCRIPTURE:
Romans 5:3-5 ESV

3.Not only that, but we rejoice in our sufferings, knowing that suffering produces endurance, 4.and endurance produces character, and character produces hope, 5.and hope does not put us to shame, because God's love has been poured into our hearts through the Holy Spirit who has been given to us.

GOD IS YOUR SOURCE

Experiencing a lengthy season of desperate financial need, which involved a calculated risk travelling from Wanaka to Glenorchy, New Zealand, for a photo shoot. The stress and pressure associated with our financial drought, after a prolonged period of unemployment, was so intense, we knew the importance of taking time out. It was time to gain ground.

Faith can be costly. It involves stepping out into the unknown, realising you are not alone, God is with you, which brings comfort. Hope is the bridge that faith is built on. Place your hope in God when your circumstances don't line up with what you are expecting.

Be impregnated with hope, in believing God will come through for you. You cannot remain stuck in fear or uncertainty when you put your trust and hope in God, every little thing will be alright, fear not. He will guide and lead you.

One step at a time. Step out. Step up. Do not look back. You are history in the making. A world changer. A champion, in Christ. Be at peace.

SCRIPTURE:
2 Corinthians 1:3-5 TPT
3.All praises belong to the God and Father of our Lord Jesus Christ. For he is the Father of tender mercy and the God of endless comfort. 4.He always comes alongside us to comfort us in every suffering so that we can come alongside those who are in any painful trial. We can bring them this same comfort that God has poured out upon us. 5.And just as we experience the abundance of Christ's own sufferings, even more of God's comfort will cascade upon us through our union with Christ.

TRIUMPHANT IN CHRIST

On a beautiful summer's day, I realised I was triumphant in Christ in overcoming everything that would attempt to restrain me and silence the voice God has given me. It was my intention, with God's help, to climb the mountain, to reach Red Tarns, Mt Cook, New Zealand, which I had trained for.

I was committed mentally and physically to the climb. But nothing prepared me for it once I started the ascent. The gradient was unimaginably steep. Of course, the pictures and maps were a guide only. From the start, every fibre of my being was stretched to capacity. But I would not surrender to defeat.

During my ascent, I grew so desperate to complete the climb, I held onto shrubs and advanced, using my hands and knees at times, to reach the top. I would not surrender to defeat, particularly as I was so close to the top. I dug deep into my faith and evidenced that all things are possible with God, in reaching the 'summit'. I can do all things through Christ Who strengthens me. And so can you.

Whatever adversity you are facing, you're not alone. God is with you. He is for you. He is working through you. Rest. Be at peace. Don't give up. Your greatest battle is evident when you are closest to your God-given breakthrough. Hold onto hope.

SCRIPTURE:
Hebrews 10:35-36 NLT
35.So do not throw away this confident trust in the Lord. Remember the great reward it brings you! 36.Patient endurance is what you need now, so that you will continue to do God's will. Then you will receive all that he has promised.

IN CHRIST, YOU ARE AN OVERCOMER

In Christ, you have the authority to trample upon serpents and scorpions. Perhaps you're in a situation, where you don't see a way out. Resist overthinking and over-talking the present. It shall pass. God is a history maker, a way maker, He has already accomplished your path to victory, supernaturally.

As a born-again believer, you have the resurrection power of Jesus dwelling on the inside of you. It's time to take authority over your circumstances. Don't give power to the situations that attempt to rule your life. Define your boundaries. Rise up in the Spirit and speak God's Word back to the devil.

You have been silent for too long. You've been trampled on mentally and emotionally, and for some, you have been physically abused, making you feel used and unwanted. You're on the brink of burn out. Stop the repetitive negative talk. Start walking and talking in your God-given authority. Claim back what is your God-given inheritance. God will restore what has been stolen from you. Trust Him.

You're standing on the threshold of something exceptional from God, do not allow the devil to attempt to confiscate it from you. Arise and shine. Come out stronger, wiser, and kinder, in Christ. This is your year of release, recovery, discovery, and restoration over circumstances that have attempted to cause you to be bruised and victimised. It's time to advance into your God-given destination.

SCRIPTURE:
Luke 10:19 NIV
I have given you authority to trample on snakes and scorpions and to overcome all the power of the enemy; nothing will harm you.

EXTRAORDINARILY YOU

Look for the extraordinary from the ordinary. God created you, as His original Masterpiece. You are as unique as your fingerprint. Perhaps your battle has been lengthy, and you are viewing life from exhaustive emotions.

Celebrate you, be a blessing. Lose sight of distractions that attempt to dismantle your God-given peace and joy. Live in the rhythm of God's heartbeat. Be still to hear His quiet whisper, and purposefully soak your soul and spirit in His peace.

Disqualify the lies from Satan that have attempted to restrict God's intentionality for you. Be free to explore, experience and expand into new directions. Stretch yourself beyond your imagination by believing God's Truth. Soak your heart in the pulse of heaven, in His Word.

Believe in your God-given instincts and pursue His purpose for your life. Forgive. Flourish. Rest.

SCRIPTURE:
Psalm 139: 13-15 AMP
13.For You formed my innermost parts; You knit me [together] in my mother's womb. 14.I will give thanks *and* praise to You, for I am fearfully and wonderfully made; wonderful are Your works, and my soul knows it very well. 15.My frame was not hidden from You, when I was being formed in secret, and intricately *and* skilfully formed [as if embroidered with many colours] in the depths of the earth.

IT'S NOT TOO LATE

Perseverance pays in every area of your life. Never give up in preparing what God has purposed for you. Particularly if you're mature I encourage you to lift your head, relax your shoulders, keep your eyes on the prize that God has intended for you to receive, and be a blessing to others.

It's never too late to live your life on purpose. Resist the lies of the devil that inform you, you're too mature. You're a champion in Christ, shake off the disappointments of what could have been, resist regret and shame. And the mantle of joyous praise instead of the spirit of heaviness. Isaiah 61:3 TPT.

Celebrate you, give thanks to God for what you have, give the little you have to Him with hope and expectancy and watch God multiply it. Life is but a vapour, do not waste time and energy. Stop cultivating the disappointments associated with your past and attempting to blend them into your present.

You're precious, life is short and fragile. Don't waste a thought on anything that could attract negativity and defeat. In Christ you matter and so does the outcome of your attitude. Be buoyant by living in faith from moment to moment. Every little thing will be okay. Be at peace always. Become all that God has assigned for you.

SCRIPTURE:
James 4:14 ESV
Yet you do not know what tomorrow will bring. What is your life? For you are a mist that appears for a little time and then vanishes.

THERE IS NO LOOKING BACK

There is hope in every circumstance. Keep your mind fixed on the things above. A silver lining always rises above every dark cloud. In your midnight hour, sing praises to God. Praise Him and you will be raised. Resist giving power to the darkness.

Perfect your perception, what are you focusing on? Be encouraged, God will equip and empower you to come through this time. What is He teaching you?

Walk into the opportunities before you, they do not beg or draw their attention to you, you need to get up and seek what appears to be hidden. Opportunities predominantly nestle neatly behind opposition. Be faith-filled and determined to succeed.

Today is a blessing from God. Don't waste time and energy on your past. It doesn't define you. Stop competing and encourage the completion of the story being told to you, by leaning into, listening, and being genuinely interested in what is being said to you, without interrupting and being better than, or more than. Competitiveness is rooted in rejection and abandonment. Stop it. In Christ, you are worthy.

Be sensitive. Be gracious. Be kind. Be genuinely interested in others. Be healed, in Jesus' Name.

SCRIPTURE:
Colossians 3:2 TPT
Yes, feast on all the treasures of the heavenly realm and fill your thoughts with heavenly realities, and not with the distractions of the natural realm.

PERSEVERE WITH COURAGE

Rest and Restoration. Separation for preparation. Are you prepared for what God has for you? Those who sow their tears as seeds will reap a harvest with joyful shouts of glee. Psalm 126:5 TPT. (A sewer weeps when he sows his precious seed while his children are hungry. This is a picture of sacrificing what little we have for the harvest to come).

Boats and ships are designed to float, and so are humans. You are created to rise above your circumstances. In Christ you are more than a conqueror. Boats and ships sink when water enters the vessel and the same principle applies to you when you permit the enemy, the devil, to penetrate and pierce your mind with his lies and deception, in an attempt to influence your life negatively.

The effects of those thoughts, if permitted, will capsise you mentally and emotionally, if you give them the power to do so. What is in you, works its way through you. Repel potentially harmful thought processes at their onset, resist sinking into discouragement. Purposefully swim upstream, be buoyant in your thinking. Strengthen and celebrate your identity, in Christ. Be encouraged. Be at peace.

When you're about to give up, God breaks through. What ripple effect are your words creating? Your thoughts shape your day and influence your destiny.

SCRIPTURE:
Proverbs 18:21 MSG
Words kill, words give life; they're either poison or fruit-you choose.

HOPE IN EVERY CIRCUMSTANCE

Hope = Healing Of Painful Emotions!
Recently I watched a group of swimmers persevere in a rip that was attempting to take them out to sea. They did not panic or surrender to procrastination. Instead, early, they realised the potential outcome. The swimmers decided in unison, that they would cautiously navigate the strong rip. Which they did, successfully. And you can do the same.

Hope in Christ is your anchor. Be expectant of a good outcome, and at the same time, hope is not a passive thought, neither does it tolerate procrastination.

Instead, hope is a spiritual muscle that is carefully and persistently cultivated, particularly when adversity is acute, and, at times, lengthy. Spend time in God's presence, read and study His Word, whilst praying and praising God, that is when His peace settles upon you and works through you.

Hope is active and directional, it is believing that God has already accomplished a good outcome, that He knows what is best for you. The battle belongs to the Lord.

SCRIPTURE:
2 Chronicles 20:15 AMP
He said, "Listen carefully, all [you people of] Judah, and you inhabitants of Jerusalem, and King Jehoshaphat. The Lord says this to you, 'Be not afraid or dismayed at this great multitude, for the battle is not yours, but God's.'

SEPARATION IN CHRIST, IS PREPARATION

Victory, in Christ. I encourage you to move forward in every area of your life. Be encouraged. Put your trust in God's promises in His Word. You were created for a time such as this. Recognise that your identity is in Christ and not in the deception and the lies of which Satan is attempting to lure you to believe.

Feed your soul and your spirit with His Word. Dig deep into God's Word to discover, to recognise and to accept His purpose for your life, enabling you to walk in His Divine purposes that He has already prepared for you.

God is wanting you to live from a place of trust. View every circumstance as an opportunity to grow in Christ, and to develop character within you. God is training you to rise above attempted intimidation, lack, fear, anxiety, and frustration. Those deadly emotions don't own you. Serve them notice. Wean yourself from them by resisting thinking and talking about circumstances that have kept you bound.

Separate yourself from the chatter. Draw into intimacy with God. Recognise your God-given talents, sharpen them and re-charter your course, heading towards a fresh start. Live on purpose for a purpose. Stop hesitating and start moving forward in Godly wisdom.

SCRIPTURE:
John 8:44 TPT
"You are the offspring of your father, the devil, and you serve your father very well, passionately carrying out his desires. He's been a murderer right from the start! He never stood with the truth, for he's full of nothing but lies-lying is his native tongue. He is a master of deception and the father of lies!"

HIGH AND LIFTED UP

From today, stop agreeing with the devil regarding your identity and your circumstances. In Christ, you are seated in heavenly places which represents authority. God created you in the perfection of His image. Celebrate you, Christ in you, the hope of glory.

Your past does not define you; nor does it represent your identity. Ask God to pour His love into your thirsty soul, drenching you with His Spirit and saturating you with His peace and joy

It is time to stop punishing yourself regarding your past. Jesus was crucified on the cross for all humanity, He defeated Satan, and cleansed humanity from sin, turn to Him and repent.

Your DNA and fingerprints are uniquely you. God never 'clones' Himself. You are fashioned in God's uniqueness. Do you recognise the beauty that God has deposited within you? In Christ you are radiant from the inside out. Arise and shine be high and lifted up. To God be the glory.

SCRIPTURE:
1 Peter 2:9 NLT
But you are not like that, for you are a chosen people. You are royal priests, a holy nation, God's very own possession. As a result, you can show others the goodness of God, for he called you out of the darkness into his wonderful light.

STAND TALL! STAND STRONG!

Stand tall. Stand strong. Immovable in Christ. Put a stake in the ground. Enter new territory that is marked by God. He is with you. He is in you. God is for you. This is not a time to consider quitting.

You've deposited too much of every ounce of your soul and fibre of your being to consider throwing in the towel. Dust yourself off. Pick yourself up. Chest out. Shoulders back. Keep walking. Take others with you.

Linger not behind the closed doors, missed opportunities or what could have been. What God is finished with is for good and sealed in the past. Do not commiserate or be tempted to wish for what could have been. It's over. No regrets. And no looking back. Do not be tempted to take revenge or to live from a mindset of unforgiveness.

Celebrate new beginnings. Look forward. Gain momentum by advancing into new territory. Prevent your past from initiating procrastination. Make yourself available to new friendships.

Let the past slip from your heart, tongue, and fingertips. You're worth more than 'that', in Christ. Pick yourself up. Those who have walked away, have done you the biggest favour. Let them go, in love. Release them. Bless them. Forgive them. Move on. Rejection represents redirection. A new life, in Christ. Re-calibrate the rhythm of your heart, with God's help.

SCRIPTURE:
Psalm 34:18 NIV
The Lord is close to the brokenhearted and saves those who are crushed in spirit.

GOD'S PEACE IN TIMES OF TURMOIL

There are moments in my life when God beckons me to travel to the ocean, which I thrive on, it's where I sense God in all His glory.

During intense moments, I draw on God's healing, soothing touch. His presence. When circumstances in my life appear to be 'circling' around me, and chaos is beckoning at my door, I stand on the shoreline, whilst witnessing God's beauty and strength, He instils peace deep within. He whispers wisdom to my spirit, as I listen to, and respond to His still, small voice.

The bigger the waves, the more concentration is involved. I use that time of strong surf to let go of the complexities of life, I cling to God. The sizeable waves are an indication of God's power and His protection, which is soothing to my soul.

It's a time of humility, rejoicing and obedience to my Creator. God is no respecter of persons, what He does for me, He will do for you, in His time. Be at peace. Seek His face and His guidance, and His peace will flow through you. Be patient. Be encouraged. Persevere in hope and faith, in Him.

SCRIPTURE:
John 14:27 AMP
Peace I leave with you; My [perfect] peace I give to you; not as the world gives do I give to you. Do not let your heart be troubled, nor let it be afraid. [Let My perfect peace calm you in every circumstance and give you courage and strength for every challenge.]

DON'T SETTLE FOR LESS THAN GOD'S BEST

God has already taken care of every minute detail of your life, supernaturally. Be anxious for nothing.

Life can be challenging, quieten your soul to hear God's still, small voice. In the stillness of the moment, settle into a gentle rhythm of going about your day in a spontaneous way, that is rhythmic, whilst resisting distractions.

In Christ, you can exchange bitter for better. Lemons, for lemonade. God is good. Always. It's not what He does, but Who He is. Your attitude and choices will determine the outcome of your circumstances.

Make wise choices, let your emotions subside before you decide. Be alert and apply discernment. Do not be coerced into making unwise choices.

Everything that appears good is not always of God. Don't second guess what you think is right, seek God's advice before you potentially make an impulsive decision. The flesh will urge you to make a sudden move. But stem the flow of those thoughts that don't align with God's Word and His will. Be still. And wait upon the Lord.

SCRIPTURE:
Isaiah 40:31 TPT
But those who entwine their hearts with Yahweh will experience divine strength. They will rise up on soaring wings and fly like eagles, run their races without growing weary, and walk through life without giving up.

DO NOT SURRENDER

Be encouraged. No matter what you're experiencing, don't give up. Stand your ground. Let the Light and Truth of Jesus Christ illuminate the deception that Satan is attempting to persuade you into believing his lies.

When the opposition is the most acute, be comforted in knowing your God-given breakthrough is imminent. Remain resilient in knowing you are going to come out of your current circumstances, stronger, wiser, and more compassionate, in Christ. Catch your breath, rest and relaxation are vital in going through the passage of testing times.

I arrived at Lake Wakatipu, Queenstown, New Zealand, without wearing my waders. I walked into the freezing cold lake and stood on sharp stones that were slightly raised above the water. Although the experience was painful, I knew the discomfort was worth it. The photo shoot was memorable.

Steady yourself in the present. Do not be anxious for anything. Trust in God. Stretch yourself. Stop doing things the same way you've always done them, expecting new results. You cannot recycle previous experiences and anticipate a new avenue of opportunities with stale thoughts. Become innovative and fresh in your thinking, with God's help.

SCRIPTURE:
Ephesians 6:13 NLT
Therefore, put on every piece of God's armor so you will be able to resist the enemy in the time of evil. Then after the battle you will still be standing firm.

DEFINING MOMENTS

A turning point in your life, or defining moments, can involve decisions that normally determine an outcome in increase, responsibilities, transition, and transformation.

Figuratively speaking, your life can be likened to transitioning from a safe 'harbour', where you have felt sheltered and comfortable. At the same time, you have outgrown living in the rhythm of comfort which attracts stagnancy.

Circumstances are changing for you, and perhaps you're resisting the relevance of stepping up and out into a new dimension of what life could look like for you.

Embracing a fresh start in so many aspects, including increasing your circle of influential people who would be healthy for your mind, stimulating it towards exponential growth, and a transition that would be transformational.

Change involves adaptability, sometimes that is easier said than done, but it's essential for your growth in specific areas of your life. The time has come to dig deep and venture forth. Going out into the deep and doing it afraid, whatever 'it' looks like for you.

Perhaps you have been safely 'anchored' for a considerable time, and you're constantly looking at alternative solutions, without making progress, as a result you have become stuck in stale thinking!

You are lacking stimulation. You're also unfulfilled and confined in your present situation. There are opportunities that involve calculated risks. And you're afraid to go forward. Procrastination has prevented you from becoming all who God has created you to be and do.

DEFINING MOMENTS

Remaining in the shallow water will keep you restricted. God commands you to cast your net on the other side of the boat. Nothing is accomplished if there is no momentum towards change. You know that.

Whatever it takes to get to the other side, God is with you, in Christ you are well able. Take the first step today of moving forward to where you deserve to be. Time is fleeting. Take the leap that will transform your life, for good, and for God.

SCRIPTURE:
Luke 5:4 TPT
Jesus sat down and taught the people from the boat. When he had finished, he said to Peter, "Now row out to deep water to cast your nets and you will have a great catch."

REACH FOR THE SKIES

Here I share a moment in time regarding God's gift to me, photography. I hope my testimony will uplift your hope and faith in God. From this time forward, I encourage you to believe what God promises in His Word. All things are possible for the one who believes and trusts [in Me]. Mark 9:23 AMP.

At the age of 53, I flew in a compact helicopter, with the doors off. It was the first time I'd been in a helicopter. What a sensational flight. We flew to Mt Tutoko Glacier, Fiordland, South Island, New Zealand. It was thrilling. I sat alongside the pilot, with the doors off, and, with God's help, I captured the unforgettable scenery.

Keith, my husband, sat behind me, videoing. We were literally skimming past sheer rock faces, viewing wondrous waterfalls, thunderous in power, and ascending with all the power that 'little' helicopter possessed, up and over a ridge of mountains. It was a sensational sensory experience.

Then a thrilling descent towards the rugged, wild coastline. My heart sat in my mouth as we witnessed the massive waves crashing against mighty rocks.

The helicopter then flew effortlessly and landed on Mt Tutoko. It was an experience of a lifetime for us. The pilot literally hoisted me from the helicopter as I was so rugged up in winter clothing.

REACH FOR THE SKIES

He firmed the helicopter on the ice and kept the engine running. I ran across the glacier, wearing a waterproof deer suit. It was a heaven on earth experience. Then, on my knees, as I turned around, I looked up, and, at that moment I knew I was born to capture God's creation through His lens.

I'm writing this message to encourage you not only to live the dream, but to occupy its reality. How, you ask? By speaking, decreeing, and believing God's Word.

He is not a God who would lie, and His Word does not return void. Nothing comes from just talking. How can it? That flight was a Godly breakthrough in learning to take the impossible in the natural and for God, His Holy Spirit, to breathe life into it.

God will do the same for you if you will invite Him into your situation that has, for some of you, been fraught with anger, frustration, fear, and anxiety. Through His Divine exchange, you can breathe easily, in an atmosphere of heavenly peace. Peace is powerful! It repels opposition.

Look up, never ever give up. Resist the chatter around you and remain steadfast in what God has purposed for your life. Step up and step out in faith, your life will be totally transformed.

SCRIPTURE:
Mark 9:23 ESV
All things are possible for one who believes.

TAMING THE TONGUE

Carefully consider your words at all times because they carry consequences. What you speak is influenced by your thought life. What, and who are you thinking about? What thoughts preoccupy your mind, from sunrise to sunset?

The mind is the battlefield. It is where Satan draws your attention first thing in the morning before your feet make contact with the floor. It is important that you put on God's Spiritual Armour early in the morning. (Ephesians 6:11-17).

Have you been rejected? Has someone cut in on your lane? Have you been overlooked for a promotion? Whatever your source of pain is, do not become poisonous or vindictive. "Vengeance is mine, I will repay, says the Lord." Romans 12:19 ESV. Seek comfort in God's presence.

Be inspirational, intentional, imaginative, intuitive, take time out to spread joy and love. Paint somebody else's day with a colourful palette of genuine affection, encouragement, and interest. Indulge your senses with laughter and every good and beautiful thing.

Jesus' extraordinary, extravagant love and grace are beyond measure. Be organic, original, and distinctive. Replace all negative thoughts and excuses with I can do all things through Him who strengthens me. (Philippians 4:13 ESV).

SCRIPTURE:
James 3:4 TPT
And the same with mighty ships, though they are massive and driven by fierce winds, yet they are steered by a tiny rudder at the direction of the person at the helm.

RISE ABOVE

Recently I received an award as Best Fine Art Landscape Photographer in Australia. Nothing comes from nothing, how can it? The discipline, determination, and faith in God as a mature Fine Art Landscape Photographer has been an exhilarating and exceptional experience.

In the following paragraphs, I outline what my world as a photographer has looked like over the passage of time. This book is not just about working through sticky situations, but it also focuses on the victory of going through and reaching the other side and being an overcomer in Christ, irrespective of how tough and challenging your circumstances are.

Standing on the front row with men from around the world at an iconic photographic location, Mesa Arch, USA, has been etched deep within my soul. Their resistance to my presence deepened my resolve to sharpen the art of Fine Art Landscape Photography. Some were nudging and pressurising me for a spot on the front row. I would not succumb to that pressure!

Stepping into icy rivers. Flying in a helicopter with the doors off. Walking 10 kilometres in waders in snake infested mountainous terrain. Standing on rocky ledges with thunderous waves rising to meet me, thrilling, and yet petrifying. Storm chasing, with clouds heavily impregnated with rain.

Narrowly avoiding stepping onto a venomous snake. Colliding with a kangaroo whilst driving my vehicle. Hiking to numerous destinations before the signs of first light. Including the sighting of a crocodile during a shoot.

RISE ABOVE

Walking through dangerous city streets with an angel guiding me, indescribable. All because God has chosen me to be His extreme Fine Art Landscape Photographer.

There have been moments when my flesh reacted when I cracked my bedding during the very early hours of the morning. I would not heed to it. All of what you have just read, has been accomplished with God's help in my mature years.

You are never alone. In some distinctly desperate, fearful moments, when I wanted to run back to the safety of my vehicle or to my hotel room. I stood on the promises of God, particularly Psalm 91. I thank God for His gift of photography to me, so it can speak to, and motivate humanity.

You have come a long way, accomplished much, fought the lion and the bear, God has equipped you to keep on galvanising your faith, in Him. You were created for a time such as this. Whatever God has put in your hand, the gifts He has given you, I encourage you to use them, to make a difference in someone else's life. Your story for God's glory.

SCRIPTURE:
Ephesians 2:10 AMP
For we are His workmanship [His own master work, a work of art], created in Christ Jesus [reborn from above-spiritually transformed, renewed, ready to be used] for good works, which God prepared [for us] beforehand [taking paths which He set], so that we would walk in them [living the good life which He prearranged and made ready for us].

CREATED FOR COMMUNITY

You and I are created for community. Satan's intention is to separate, divide and discourage you in an attempt to weaken your relationships: family, friends, and colleagues, primarily through offense, bitterness, resentment and unforgiveness.

It is the devil's purpose for humanity to live a life representing a repetitive cycle of isolation and torment. And usually, the root cause of isolation is rejection and abandonment, of course, it could be various scenarios for different people.

Satan's purposes and plans are to wound humanity with words, so that you hibernate in seclusion, and you withdraw with a wounded soul, otherwise recognised as isolation. The heart freezes over from icy thoughts. Only God's love can thaw your broken heart.

You need to surrender your grief, sorrow, and other deadly emotions that are present in your soul, which are attempting to grip your mind, and heart, and ask God to heal your woundedness. Do not surrender to the wiles of Satan. Speak God's Word. Stand your ground. Walk from a posture of victory. God never leaves you nor forsakes you!

SCRIPTURE:
Ecclesiastes 4: 9-12 NLT
9.Two people are better off than one, for they can help each other succeed. 10.If one person falls, the other can reach out and help. But someone who falls alone is in real trouble. 11.Likewise, two people lying close together can keep each other warm. But how can one be warm alone? 12.A person standing alone can be attacked and defeated, but two can stand back-to-back and conquer. Three are even better, for a triple-braided cord is not easily broken.

THE JOY OF THE LORD IS YOUR STRENGTH

Laughter heals. It sustains, strengthens and stabilisers you. Joy is God's delight in you. It is God in heaven informing you that every little thing is going to be alright. Joy is heaven invading earth. Keep the main thing the main thing. And don't sweat the small stuff. Be wise in whom you confide in.

Let Godly wisdom resonate in your spirit. Timing is everything, God's perfect timing. Joy that bubbles up from deep within you and overflows, and releases healing in your soul. Laughter is God's Spiritual prescription for you. It informs Satan of your identity in Christ.

Joy reminds the devil, the battle has been won, in Christ. It's in the unseen, and the not knowing, that if permitted, can unravel you. Do not give the enemy power. You possess authority in Christ, walk in it daily. You have everything to gain.

Christ in you, is unrivalled, soak in God's Truth about you. God's love is for you, you're the apple of His eye. Your laughter resonates in receiving His love. It represents victory. Resist distractions they are a lie from Satan, it's his plan to weaken, overwhelm and to exhaust you.

Joy is strength in God. It is contagious. A heart filled with joy changes the atmosphere in a room. It navigates through troubled waters with Divine direction, clarity, and peace.

Cultivate the Spirit of joy by opening your heart and spirit to God as He pours His love into you and transforms your life from heaviness to the lightness of your innermost being.

THE JOY OF THE LORD IS YOUR STRENGTH

Rise up. Run to the battle line as David did with Goliath. Confront the lies and deception that you have believed for too long. Joy is confirmation of trusting God in every situation, that the outcome is exceedingly above and beyond what you could imagine.

Joy is taking your hands off other people's lives; in attempting to change them, it resists control and manipulation. Joy looks at life with love and covers potential offences, and enquires what can be done to bring healing, in Christ.

In its purest form, joy, is God reaching out to you, and healing your heart, with the grace of God enabling you to laugh at your mistakes and to settle differences, in His peace. Whilst God delights in giving you the desires of your heart.

SCRIPTURE:
Nehemiah 8:10 NIV
Nehemiah said, "Go and enjoy choice food and sweet drinks, and send some to those who have nothing prepared. This day is holy to our Lord. Do not grieve, for the joy of the Lord is your strength."

FORGIVENESS LIBERATES

If you're facing a battle today that appears insurmountable, I encourage you to possess a posture of trusting God. All things are possible, only believe. Your story for His glory. Forgive. Love. Laugh.

No day is the same. Stop 're-treading' your yesteryears. Let go of the guilt and shame, give your pain to God, resist replaying the torment in thoughts that enlarge the original scenario. Forgive others. Forgive yourself. Increase, influence, and impartation, in Christ. Only believe.

Your thoughts, first thing in the morning, create a ripple effect for the day. Live in the miracle of today. You cannot allow your flesh to dictate your decisions. Life is precious. Time is priceless. Spend it wisely. You cannot buy it back.

Live in the unforced rhythms of God's grace. Stop striving, God's timing is perfect. Get off the treadmill of perfection and 'overdoing'. Purposely step into the promises of God which are "yes" and "amen". And plead the Blood of Jesus Christ over everything that has attempted to steal, kill, and destroy your present/future. It is time to let go and let God.

SCRIPTURE:
Ephesians 4:32 AMP
Be kind and helpful to one another, tender-hearted [compassionate, understanding], forgiving one another [readily and freely], just as God in Christ also forgave you.

FACING YOUR GIANTS

Perhaps your greatest moment involves a giant leap of faith. I encourage you to believe in what God has already prepared for you and to go forward unafraid as He is in you, with you, and working miracles through you.

Do not let go of your faith in God, it will propel you into something exceptional. Be encouraged. Be at peace. Be inspired. Go and explore new opportunities and avenues that will take you to another space and place, in Christ.

Run to the battle line, as David did with Goliath. As Goliath moved closer to attack, David quickly ran out to meet him. 1 Samuel 17:48 NLT. Challenge the giants with God's Word and inform them of how big God is.

When you stand on God's promises, by decreeing and believing in His Word over your circumstances, God will whisper relevant strategies to you in overcoming them. Complicated situations will no longer have a hold over your life. And His peace will be restored.

In Christ, by God's grace, you can conquer circumstances that have appeared too big or intimidating, and by speaking His Word, you can overcome all of Satan's strategies which have attempted to keep you bound in fear. Inform Satan he no longer has a hold over your life.

Embrace new beginnings. Occupy the reality of your God-given dreams and destiny, which will bring fulfilment and purpose into every facet of your life and transform the lives of those around you.

FACING YOUR GIANTS

Speak and declare God's Word over your situation, until you witness His Word doing a good work in and through you and those around you. Some of whom you have been praying for, and perhaps, for a considerable time.

The Bible is transformational, and God's Word never returns void. It is the same with my word. I send it out, and it always produces fruit. It will accomplish all I want it to, and it will prosper everywhere I send it. Isaiah 55:11 NLT.

Your life in Christ is all who God created you to be. Live it, be it, let Him inhabit and possesses you. Go with new ideas and adventures, grow in faith. Choices are to be made. Don't miss a golden opportunity to step into something extraordinary that God has already prepared for you.

I remember watching a world record holder at the Olympics, who thought she had her gold medal in the 'bag' but she gave it away due to complacency. Do not permit Satan to snatch what God has purposed for your life. Be vigilant. Always.

Never give up. Never give in, in believing in God.

SCRIPTURE:
Isaiah 41:10 TPT
Do not yield to fear, for I am always near. Never turn your gaze from me, for I am your faithful God. I will infuse you with my strength and help you in every situation. I will hold you firmly with my victorious right hand.

Today, this moment in time, God is with you, in you (born again believers), and working through you. Today is history for God, nothing can startle or surprise Him. Jesus overcame everything on the cross. His resurrection power that resides within you, arrests, and binds that which is opposing you.

He canceled out every legal violation we had on our record and the old arrest warrant that stood to indict us. He erased it all-our sins, our stained soul-he deleted it all and they cannot be retrieved! Everything we once were in Adam has been placed onto his cross and nailed permanently there as a public display of cancellation. Colossians 2:14 TPT.

In Christ, you are more than a conqueror. Stand up. Stand out. Speak up. Speak out. Do not permit pressure from people to silence you or influence you to withdraw from where God has positioned you.

Sometimes, they don't understand the journey God has planned for your life. Apply Godly wisdom in whom you speak to regarding what God has put on your heart. Resist approval addiction, it can be emotionally costly.

To be honest, without being poisonous, It is not always a smooth ride, when making choices that align with God's will for your life as you may experience interruptions from those around you. Focus on Jesus, let everything slide off you.

Deal with them in kindness. Develop boundaries, but not walls. Otherwise, you wall yourself in and others out. That way of living is unhealthy. Relationships in life are vital. Almost as much as your heartbeat. I mention this without hinting on co-dependency.

Be content where God has you at present. Look forward and plan, one step ahead at a time to where God intends you to be. Be at peace. The joy of the Lord is your strength. Laughter that 'permeates', (a sweet scent of Heaven), representing an atmosphere filled with God's love!

14.But thanks be to God, who always leads us in triumph in Christ, and through us spreads *and* makes evident everywhere the sweet fragrance of the knowledge of Him. 15.For we are the *sweet* fragrance of Christ [which ascends] to God, [discernible both] among those who are being saved and among those who are perishing, 2 Corinthians 2:14-15 AMP.

SCRIPTURE:
Deuteronomy 31:6 MSG
"Be strong. Take courage. Don't be intimidated. Don't give them a second thought because God, your God Is striding ahead of you. He's right there with you. He won't let you down; he won't leave you."

AGAINST ALL ODDS, STAND FIRM

If you are experiencing opposition, read on. This message outlines my experience as a photographer in weather conditions that were extreme, whilst shooting at an iconic location. I prayed for calm conditions. God knows what is best for you, and for me.

The afternoon that I made my way to Dragon's Head, Mornington Peninsula, Australia, for a photo shoot, the wind whipped strongly against me, and the rain was relentless. I wore waders whilst I made my way to this incredible location with my tutor. It was a considerable walk, with the beach sand crunching under our feet. I was exhausted when I reached Dragon's Head.. As we approached the impressive rock shelf, I noticed the tide was coming in.

When we arrived at the rock shelf, the wind and rain were pitching everything at us. I was carrying my camera and tripod. Walking on the rock shelf felt as though I was walking in a field of land mines as it had numerous deep potholes.

Initially the opposition due to the weather conditions was intense. My tripod and camera were secured on the rock. I stood my ground. I would not surrender to the wind and the rain beating against my body and attempting to saturate my camera.

As my soul quietened, I observed, with the incoming tide, the waves were impressive in size as they accelerated towards me. Initially, the waves were intimidating. But then I recognised their momentum. I navigated amongst the deep potholes, by leapfrogging them, and, at times, stumbling into them. I was gaining ground with quiet confidence.

AGAINST ALL ODDS, STAND FIRM

My tutor and I stood in the pouring rain. An umbrella was ineffective in keeping my camera and filters dry. A thought ran through my mind, turn back, and run for cover and warmth. NO way! There was no alternative but to persevere with my shoot.

Whilst I continued through the storm, peace came over me as I knew God had His hand upon me as I realised those were the conditions He wanted me to experience. The rising tide was amazing, I continued to stand and watch, with fascination, as the water rushed towards me. With God's peace I was able to break through the fear barrier and rise to another level in my photography.

My testimony is this: God revealed my life to me during that afternoon, He was ever present, walking through the years of storms. He was taking me to a place of peace, victory and shining His light, as He always has, but this time I saw its significance for the first time in my life.

Everything that afternoon was a film strip, a vision of my life. I was living in His Light, Truth, peace and from His victory. Never give up and never surrender to the lies of the devil. With God all things are possible, only believe. Keep your gaze on Him. I have written these words to encourage you to build hope in your situation.

SCRIPTURE:
2 Corinthians 4:8 AMP
We are pressured in every way [hedged in] but not crushed; perplexed [unsure of finding a way out], but not driven to despair.

CONSIDER YOUR OPTIONS

In life there are so many choices and decisions to be made. Sometimes, it can be almost overwhelming when you need to make choices that will eventuate into a good outcome.

It is at this time of decision-making that you need to quieten your soul and to hear from God. The flesh is unpredictable and fickle. It wants its demands satisfied and does not consider some potentially serious consequences if the inappropriate decision is made.

Options are choices in the making. Sometimes, the availability of what is in front of you, is not always easy to distinguish between the right path or the wrong one.

In a moment of quietness, give your soul time to experience peace. God's peace is your umpire. His peace will enable you to navigate safely through your decision-making. In life, there are major decisions to be considered, either for promotion, relocating to another State or country or what school or college to send your child to.

What may appear insignificant in your decision-making if you are impulsive, could result in something more complicated than you could imagine. Resist making hasty decisions. It's important to read the small print, be attentive to what you are absorbing regarding facts. Do your research and be prepared. Preparation is prevention and precaution.

SCRIPTURE:
James 1:5 ESV
If any of you lacks wisdom, let him ask God, who gives generously to all without reproach, and it will be given him.

A FRESH NEW START

When you become comfortable in your life, stagnancy and status quo are likely to set in. But its paradoxical, as so often when you're established in your ways, you also want to move to higher ground, to focus on new frontiers from what you have become so accustomed to. You lack the motivation to do so. And sometimes fear can freeze your thinking from gaining momentum in leaving that which lies behind.

There is a battle in your mind between being comfortable and the process of adaptability regarding a new way of life, a stimulating environment and meeting new friends. Change far outweighs the mundane of remaining the same. As I write this, I'm not championing relocating annually to a new home, or the like, but distinguish when your thoughts and attitude are stagnated.

Choose to challenge yourself in gaining knowledge in your professional sphere of influence, or to improve your abilities regarding hobbies you are interested in. Knowledge is power. It equips you to deepen your knowledge and to become a mentor to someone and encourage them to grow.

What you have spoken over your life is where you are today, but you don't need to remain there. It is time for you to build yourself up in the Lord and to move onwards and upwards, to a life that is fulfilling and purposeful.

SCRIPTURE:
Ecclesiastes 3:1 NIV
There is a time for everything, and a season for every activity under the heavens.

LIFE IS PRICELESS

From this moment, I encourage you to live from a posture of rest in Christ, as you are seated in heavenly places with Him. Dwell in His presence. Live extravagantly in Christ, as He pours His love into you, and for you to receive and to respond to His love.

There is no need for you to attempt to impress anyone to be recognised. Approval addiction and co-dependency are rooted in wanting to be loved and acknowledged.

The person or people whom you are attempting to gain recognition from, may, either never pay you the attention you are seeking, or perhaps they may move past you without recognising your God-given abilities. And that can hurt.

Misconception so often results in rejection. To be honest, humanity is entitled to have their opinion that differs from your point of view. They are not necessarily rejecting you. Take an inventory regarding the repetitive incidents that have caused you to be 'stung' by words that may not have been intended to harm you. And you have reacted by withdrawing.

Perhaps you have been overcommitted and you are exhausted. Fatigue can squeeze the life from you. It is imperative to live life in a balanced way. Separate yourself from the almost overwhelming schedule you have committed yourself to and recognise the areas that you need to deal with, regarding being overcommitted.

As you reflect the image of God, you recognise that there is no need for competitiveness, or living from a spirit of inferiority and inadequacy.

LIFE IS PRICELLESS

Everything you need for this life; you have in Christ. He is your Source, in every facet of who you are, and in your requirements. In Christ, you are priceless. I encourage you to recognise what God has deposited within you.

See yourself as God created you, in His image, for His purpose. For His glory. In Christ, nothing is wasted. Rise above your regrets, shame, guilt, disappointment, despondency, or any other negative, deadly emotions. Surrender your heart to God, trust Him in healing your hurt and pain.

Let it go. How? By forgiving and re-chartering your thoughts with good thoughts. Refrain from giving power to those who persecute you. Bless them. Do not curse them.

Allow God's soothing Spirit to saturate your soul. Go forward unafraid as God is with you and in you, and for you. Be at peace. You are precious, beautiful and a delight to Him. You are closer to your breakthrough than you can imagine. Hold fast to your faith. God is your deliverer. Shalom.

SCRIPTURE:
Philippians 4:6-7 AMP
6.Do not be anxious or worried about anything, but in everything [every circumstance and situation] by prayer and petition with thanksgiving, continue to make your [specific] requests known to God. 7.And the peace of God [that peace which reassures the heart, that peace] which transcends all understanding, [that peace which] stands guard over your hearts and minds in Christ Jesus [is yours].

BE STILL YOUR BEATING HEART

Soothing. Serene. Serendipity. Be still your beating heart. In the stillness of the moment, inhale the inspiration of God's creation. Reflect on what God is putting on your heart to bring change in your life, which so often represents healing.

Ask, and thank God to revive your soul that is sagging due to stress and endless, lengthy days of commitments. Ask and thank Him to restore the years the locusts have eaten. What do 'locusts' represent to you? Join your faith with God and watch His Spirit move to transform your life, from ordinary to extraordinary as you cultivate your hope in God. And, as you transition from old mindsets to new ways of thinking, in Christ.

Walk into every opportunity, with intentionality, and thrive. Live on purpose for a purpose. It's so easy to talk about change and new beginnings but change always involves commitment. You cannot become fit by simply discussing exercise. It involves discipline and a desire to change to another gear in your thinking, and accelerating towards new goals, which need to be set.

Purposefully connect with someone who will keep you accountable. Decline invitations associated with negativity. Pursue God's peace. A new day, a new way, a new life. Rest your mind. Deliberately step across the line into your destiny. The only person holding you back is yourself. Stop it.

SCRIPTURE:
Joel 2:25 NLT
The Lord says, "I will give you back what you lost to the swarming locusts, the hopping locusts, the stripping locusts, and the cutting locusts. It was I who sent this great destroying army against you."

HEALING FOR THE HURTING

Roll away the stone. What does your 'stone' represent? God has put on my heart to ask you to roll away the stone, associated with past hurts, failures, etcetera, and to come out from the shadows. You have been hiding for too long.

John 11:43 Jesus shouted with a loud voice, "Lazarus come out!" 44.Jesus said to them, "Unwrap him and release him." John 11:43-44 AMP. It is time to come clean and to ask God to help you identify the root causes of your issues.

Only God can heal you. Put your hand in God's hand and ask Him to heal your brokenness. You cannot do it in your own strength. God wanted to 'showcase' His glory amongst the doubters and His intention was to raise Lazarus from the dead.

He wants to do the same for you. Stop limping with past hurts that are weighing you down. Get up, get out and draw near to God. You are created in His image for a time such as this. You are more than a conqueror, in Christ. Rise up and claim your Divine Inheritance.

You are beautiful, and you add value everywhere you go. God will give you beauty for ashes, the oil of joy for mourning and a garment of praise for the spirit of heaviness. Be the difference God has created you to be and be at peace.

SCRIPTURE:
Isaiah 61:3 NIV
And provide for those who grieve in Zion-to bestow on them a crown of beauty instead of ashes, the oil of joy instead of mourning, and a garment of praise instead of a spirit of despair.

PUSHING THROUGH FEAR

I hope my testimony will uplift your hope and faith in God. The city: Florence, Italy, where God enabled me to win a prize for the gift He has given me, photography. Before daybreak, I stepped out onto the streets of Florence. The destination for my photo shoot was Piazzale Michelangelo, which is renowned for its fabulous vista of Florence.

My camera bag was on my back and my tripod was secure in my arms. I stepped out onto the streets before dawn and encountered young people overflowing from the nightclubs. I was terrified, but I knew God was with me.

Through the arterial network of cobbled streets, I blended in the dark wearing black clothing, I drew closer to the 100 steps to reach the top of Piazzale Michelangelo.

In that district, I also walked past nightclubs, whilst asking and praising God for protection as I surreptitiously 'slid' through the dark alley ways. I was literally frozen in fear. But I would not surrender to the lies of Satan, FEAR = False Evidence Appearing Real.

When I climbed the stairs, I noticed three inebriated men standing in the area I intended shooting from. Two policemen were onlookers to their antics. It was at that moment I needed to intercept and step into what God had asked me to do, my shoot. I would not withdraw or walk away due to fear. But my heart was pounding in my chest. I gesticulated to the Police to remove them. They found the men's antics amusing.

PUSHING THROUGH FEAR

With faith, I made my way to the area where the men were standing. Raising my tripod legs, I made it clear I was about to capture the city of Florence from where they were positioned. It did not take the men long to realise it was time for them to move, and they did so, quickly, and quietly.

First light had split the sky, and I was ready to start my photo shoot. Go forward unafraid, in Christ. Inform your mountains how big God is. Push through fear as the Israelites did when they walked through the Red Sea into victory.

It took strong faith and great courage walking through those mighty walls of water on either side of them. The Israelites kept looking ahead to the purposes and plans God had assigned for them.

They would not surrender to the fear that was attempting to weaken their faith. They fed their faith and starved their fear by looking straight ahead and trusting God.

SCRIPTURE:
2 Timothy 1:7 ESV
For God gave us a spirit not of fear but of power and love and self-control.

DO IT AFRAID

I hope my testimony will uplift your hope and faith in God. I had spent a considerable amount of time preparing myself for a photo shoot in Central Park, New York City, which involved walking the streets of New York City on my own, during the early hours of the morning. Although I was afraid, I knew God was with me.

The biggest step was preparing my mind for the trip ahead and disciplining myself to enter the streets as soon as possible otherwise fear would have overtaken me, if I had permitted it to. But I did not.

Turning each corner onto another street was met with acute anxiety, and an accelerated heart rate, because I never knew what, or who was before me. But God did.

You can speak the Word, but what is vital is the Word of God working through you, by His grace, as you strengthen your faith.

Before leaving the hotel for that photo shoot, I familiarised myself with the route to Central Park. Catching the Subway train was an experience all on its own. I was terrified.

Travelling to Central Park was a big adventure, packed with memorable moments, however, the importance of knowing where I was going to do my shoot from, was just as relevant. The map of Central Park became more familiar as I studied it. As always, God led me to the perfect spot.

Arriving at my location involved blending in with the darkness, wearing black clothing, until I felt safe enough to emerge and to start my shoot.

DO IT AFRAID

Nothing comes from nothing. How can it? I was 56 when I first experienced Central Park on my own. To God be the glory. What an adventurous journey. It's not too late. You're not too old. Your best years are yet ahead of you. Do it afraid. Shalom.

SCRIPTURE:
Philippians 4:13 AMP
I can do all things [which He has called me to do] through Him who strengthens and empowers me [to fulfill His purpose-I am self-sufficient in Christ's sufficiency; I am ready for anything and equal to anything through Him who infuses me with inner strength and confident peace.]

TODAY IS A GIFT

I encourage you to rejoice in the present. Today is a gift from God, I urge you to unwrap its wonderful moments, bit by bit. Every minute is a miracle, each moment, momentous. Seize the day. Perhaps, you are asking, how can I enjoy today, you don't know my circumstances? No, I don't. I sense your unspoken words. But God does.

Be rest assured, you can walk in agreement with nostalgia and live in the rear-view mirror of your past, which is a trick of Satan to remind you of your past and whatever it was packed with.

But you need to decide to trust God, you have experienced layers of pain due to re-living the same incidents that have attracted torment, and encouraged Satan to attempt to steal, kill and destroy God's plans for your life, (John 10:10). God has prepared a future filled with hope for you, Jeremiah 29:11.

You cannot live in the 'replica' of your yesteryears and expect something new to happen to you. It is time for you to put the brake on situations that have controlled your thinking for far too long.

Without finger-pointing, you have permitted people to tread on you repeatedly, until you have become vulnerable. It is time to pick up your mat, as it is written in John 5:5-8, and to be healed by God from incidents that have kept you bound in your past.

I have written this previously; perhaps some people in your life do not want you to make progress as they prefer to have you on their potter's wheel. It is time to stand up and to develop your voice in a Godly way and to apply Godly authority and express, in God's love, that you are no longer going to participate in that controlled environment.

TODAY IS A GIFT

At times, you thrive on discussing the good old days. How good were they? It is appropriate to let go of what lies behind. It does not mean that you let go of good friends, Life is a consistent rhythm of change. You need to evolve with it. God's timing is perfect.

It is time to make plans for what God is speaking to you and your heart about. Be still and know that I am God, Psalm 46:10, NIV. What you thought was impossible, the presence of God has already broken through for you. Your breakthrough is as close as God's breath upon you. Be at peace. Be encouraged.

SCRIPTURE:
Philippians 3:13-14 TPT
13.I don't depend on my own strength to accomplish this; however, I do have one compelling focus: I forget all of the past as I fasten my heart to the future instead. 14.I run straight for the divine invitation of reaching the heavenly goal and gaining the victory-prize through the anointing of Jesus.

HOLD ONTO HOPE

Here, I share a moment in time regarding God's gift to me, photography. I hope my testimony will uplift your hope and faith in God.

Capturing my image, Transition, on the Sunshine Coast, involved separating my bedding during the early hours of the morning and travelling to an area that was unfamiliar to me.

At the twelfth hour, I discovered the address I had put in the GPS, was about 500 metres off course from where I needed to be. My first thought was to panic. But I knew God's peace would overcome the mistake I'd made.

Satan was whispering to me, just give up, it's too late. With that lie, I asked the Holy Spirit to guide me to the car park where I needed to be. And He did, straight away. I was at peace, even though the light was evolving into a full sunrise.

With speed, I put on my waders, and accelerated to the location, it was my first visit there, so I was unfamiliar with the territory.

I knew the importance of keeping a 'cool' head. Following the pathway, I noticed a steep, deeply grooved path that led through some growth. I'm always aware of snakes, but I knew I needed to push through that fear.

Climbing over a fairly high fence involved some gymnastics, I soon recognised the familiar path other photographers had created and used.

HOLD ONTO HOPE

By that time, the light was full on in front of me. Instead of panicking, I sought the guidance of the Holy Spirit, whilst I secured my camera onto my tripod and immediately started shooting, with not a second to waste.

God blessed me with a sunrise that pierced the sky with splashes of colour, whilst He enabled me to extract every second of light. It was a shoot to remember.

Hold onto hope. If you're in a precarious situation, God, His Spirit, is your GPS. Do not waste energy or your health living in anger, anxiety, dread, fear, or any other deadly emotion that intends holding you back, which would like to keep you hidden and to maintain your silence.

Do not permit the devil to possess power over your life. Walk in the authority God has given you. You were created for a time such as this. Rise up. Make your move, in Christ.

SCRIPTURE:
Isaiah 26:3 NLT
You will keep in perfect peace all who trust in you, all whose thoughts are fixed on you!

WHAT ARE YOU WAITING FOR?

Here, I share a moment in time regarding God's gift to me, photography. I hope my testimony will uplift your hope and faith in God.

God gave me an opportunity to stand with all the male photographers and enjoy a photo shoot, at Mesa Arch, Canyonlands National Park, Utah, USA, which is an iconic photographic location, where photographers from around the world gather to capture a sunrise.

When I arrived before dawn at Mesa Arch, the atmosphere was intense and charged with tension. I was the fourth person to stake my tripod on the rock and to secure my position.

The welcome was a frozen silence, particularly being a woman photographer amongst the men on the front row. I did not flinch; I set my focus on my intentionally and that was to capture out of the ordinary images at a location that has been saturated with photographers for the longest time.

Just before dawn, photographers descended upon the area with head lamps, jumping over scrubby bushes, clamouring for the front row. I was firm in my stand and did not permit subtle pushing in, in fact, it came to a measure of serious intertwining of tripods.

What you put in, is what you get out. I was up early, arrived early, so, I stood my ground. As dawn cracked across the horizon, the atmosphere became more intense as shutter releases erupted around me with a sense of urgency.

WHAT ARE YOU WAITING FOR?

I continued to set my gaze on the sunrise and not on the bumping and pushing that was happening around me. I would not be distracted by the boisterous activity close by.

During my time on that photo shoot, I remained standing strong. As the sun strengthened and the photo frenzy increased, I quietly removed my camera from my tripod and freely captured interesting shots from different angles.

It is what you do with what you have in your possession, your God-given tools. I resisted succumbing to the intimidation and distractions that were whirling around me. You can do the same. With God all things are possible.

Be expectant, that something good is about to happen to you. The point I'm making is the importance of being prepared. When you plan and prepare your next move, whatever it involves, you will gain momentum and make progress to where God intends you to be.

This message is not just about photography, it's about your perspective, particularly when things don't go your way, and neither in the time frame you considered it to happen in. God is always on time.

If you're between a rock and a hard place, Jesus is your Rock. He can move mountains if you invite Him into your sticky situation, you could become unstuck with His help. Jesus' Light and Truth releases peace deep within your soul, whilst you keep the main thing, the main thing.

WHAT ARE YOU WAITING FOR?

After the photo shoot a large gathering of photographers expressed their joy in that moment. And some, including Keith, my husband, and myself, walked across the arch. It took great courage to do that, but it was worth it.

And you can do the same thing in difficult circumstances that appear impossible for you to dig yourself out of, God is your Way Maker. Trust Him. He is with you. God is working through you. And God is for you. Be expectant of a good outcome. Stop procrastinating and start moving. Shalom.

SCRIPTURE:
Deuteronomy 31:8 NIV
The Lord himself goes before you and will be with you; he will never leave you nor forsake you. Do not be afraid; do not be discouraged.

YOU CANNOT GIVE UP NOW!

Here, I share a moment in time regarding God's gift to me, photography. I hope my testimony will uplift your hope and faith in God.

Recently, I was on the road at 2.15am, driving to Fingal Head in Northern New South Wales, Australia. Cruising down the motorway in my vehicle was relaxing as the traffic was light, and the road conditions were perfect.

During the entire trip, my mind was playing a repetitive scene involved with arriving at Fingal Head car park in the dark. It is an isolated location and dread rose in me, as I knew I was on my own. But, at the same time, I was aware God was with me. The battle was to overcome dread, fear, and anxiety.

When I arrived at Fingal Head car park, it was so dark, I could barely see my hands in front of me without a head lamp on. Fear and anxiety came knocking at the door of my heart, but I refused them entry.

I disciplined myself to exit my vehicle straight away. I put my camera bag on my back and carried my tripod whilst I started walking towards the ocean. In the past, procrastination held me frozen in fear, due to the dark and thick bush, when I had chosen to return to the safety of my vehicle. But not this time, I was determined to go forward afraid.

Isn't it amazing, or annoying, how your mind can make a mountain out of a molehill, that is rooted in fear? The fear originated from who could be in the bush and attack me.

YOU CANNOT GIVE UP NOW!

God reminded me of a picture walking with Jesus, the Lion, from the Tribe of Judah. I spoke the Word and held that image in my mind of Jesus and the Lion with each step, as I walked through dense bush in the dark. It took every ounce of faith to reach my destination before dawn. Anything that is worth fighting for, you know is going to be exceptional.

The climb down the steep muddy bank, with rugged rocks involved courage and intentionality, whilst walking in the dark, with a head lamp partially covered as I didn't want anyone to know I was there, that is what drives me.

Walking relentlessly to my location in fear. Yet, not surrendering to fear and witnessing the compelling experience during my shoot in stimulating locations, I know is worth it.

It was thrilling witnessing the huge waves accelerating towards me. The area I worked from was steep, slippery, and potentially dangerous when the water and spray saturated me and my equipment. As it is with every other photographic destination, the importance of arriving early is paramount.

God is good and faithful. I always walk away from potentially dangerous places like Fingal Head, with a spring in my step because I know God has protected me. And He does the same for you.

To accomplish what God has prepared for you involves walking in faith, sometimes, big steps of leaning into God. Drawing close to Him in intimacy.

YOU CANNOT GIVE UP NOW!

Faith is love in action, in believing and trusting in God's promises. It is a case of walking by faith and not by sight. So we don't look at the troubles we can see now; rather, we fix our gaze on things that cannot be seen. For the things we see now will soon be gone, but the things we cannot see will last forever, 2 Corinthians 4:18 NLT.

The sunrise was extraordinary, and God enabled me to appreciate Him on my own as it is an iconic photographic location where photographers jostle for a good vantage point. I get that.

Be hopeful. Be joyous. Be intentional about moving forward. You cannot give up now. The testing times are when God purifies you. You have come too far to surrender to fear and to the lies of Satan. God is waiting for you to move, step by step towards your God-given destiny.

SCRIPTURE:
1 Peter 1:6-7 ESV
6.In this you rejoice, though now for a little while, if necessary, you have been grieved by various trials, 7.so that the tested genuineness of your faith-more precious than gold that perishes though it is tested by fire-may be found to result in praise and glory and honor at the revelation of Jesus Christ.

If you are experiencing loneliness, or perhaps you have been wounded by words that pierce your heart and soul, you have a sense of being abandoned, rejected, overlooked, or unappreciated. Perhaps you are in a desperate situation, whether it be finances, relationships, or health, know that God is right beside you. He is closer than a breath away.

When you are vulnerable, tired and have experienced a battle for a lengthy period, Satan tempts humanity with lies and deception, which is a trap that you need to be aware of. Ask God for discernment and clarity, for a sharpness of His Spirit communicating with your spirit, become receptive to His still, small voice.

As it is written in God's Word, The thief comes only in order to steal and kill and destroy. I came that they may have and enjoy life, and have it in abundance [to the full, till it overflows]. John 10:10 AMP. When you are alone, although God is always with you, you can become vulnerable to the empty threats of the devil.

As a lion seeks its prey, it immediately looks for the weak animal that's not travelling in a 'pack'. God's Word says in 1 Peter 5:8-9 AMP, 8.Be sober [well balanced and self-disciplined], be alert and cautious at all times. That enemy of yours, the devil, prowls around like a roaring lion [fiercely hungry], seeking someone to devour. 9.But resist him, be firm in your faith [against his attack-rooted, established, immovable], knowing that the same experiences of suffering are being experienced by your brothers and sisters throughout the world. [You do not suffer alone.}

IN YOUR TIME OF NEED

Isolation, resulting from a decision to withdraw from society due to a wounded soul, which is rooted in rejection, and results in loneliness. Initially isolation appears to be the solution, or a way out, of being free from being ignored, rejected, or verbally abused. It feels safe not to have contact with people, but loneliness is not the solution.

Some individuals have an unbalanced need to always be surrounded by people, it's their solution to attempt to distract themselves from their emotional pain deep within their soul. But you can be in a room crowded with people you know, and still feel lonely and unfulfilled.

There are circumstances that involve intended feelings and emotions to dismantle your peace and joy, in Christ, but you cannot succumb to the wiles of the evil one.

If you permit Satan to, he will separate and torment you, with poisonous, deadly emotions. Every day, in each circumstance you require God's advice, suggestions, strategies and solutions to live from His victory.

Perhaps you have chosen to separate yourself to gain strength, I urge you to have someone you can trust, to come alongside you. It is not God's intention for His children to live life, stressed, strained, struggling and tormented, barely getting by, and living isolated.

IN YOUR TIME OF NEED

You are wise in Christ, precious, a gift from God. You are a solution to someone's complex situation. Push forward. Let go of your exhaustive emotions by trusting God, and by being intentional and slowing your pace.

Sometimes burn out can be a result of attending excessively to the needs of others, whilst neglecting to rest and to live a slower pace where you require to be refreshed. Be balanced. Be blessed. Be at peace. Shalom.

SCRIPTURE:
1 John 4:16 AMP
We have come to know [by personal observation and experience], and have believed [with deep, consistent faith] the love which God has for us. God is love, and the one who abides in love abides in God, and God abides continually in him.

COME CLEAN BEFORE GOD

Emotions are fickle and unpredictable. Words spoken in love today are intended to set you on the right course, yet, tomorrow, the same words could represent offence to you, or other similar emotions that you could react to.

What are your 'trigger' mechanisms? What are the things that you react to? What are the root causes of those emotions that 'trigger' you into a state of frustration, anger, or any other host of emotions that introduce tension?

This message is not intended to point a finger at you. But time is fleeting, the years go by so quickly, and whatever is eating at you, can only be solved, and healed by being honest with God, ask for His healing touch to transform your life. Forgive those you are angry with.

Anger and other harmful emotions not only introduce an unpleasant atmosphere in your home, which is stressful, but they influence your health. God, His Spirit, is your revealer and healer.

Seek His face and ask God to reveal to you the pain that is buried deep within your soul. Bitterness, resentment and unforgiveness develop roots which, when surrendered to God, He can bring healing to your soul and release His peace to you, and through you.

It is time for you to wean yourself from the influence of your flesh, and its demands, and for you to live from the Fruit of God's Spirit.

22.But the Holy Spirit produces this kind of fruit in our lives: love, joy, peace, patience, kindness, goodness, faithfulness, 23.gentleness and self-control. There is no law against these things! Galatians 5:22-23 NLT.

COME CLEAN BEFORE GOD

I encourage you to deal with situations that have caused you to run from being healed by God. Also, to confront root causes which have controlled you, which attract frustration, anxiety, fear, regret, shame, and guilt, as already mentioned.

Forgiveness is freedom from a victim mentality, releasing you from mental torment. When you forgive, you're no longer held captive in your mind. And you've set the other individual/s free too, in Christ.

You were created for a time such as this. You stand out in an exceptional way, for every right and good reason. You can go forward and live in God's peace. Live, laugh and love as you never have before.

It's time to put a stop to the things that have been stealing your joy and peace. Turn the other cheek, let go and let God. Be at peace. You can do it, in Christ Jesus.

SCRIPTURE:
Ephesians 4:26-27 TPT
26.But don't let the passion of your emotions lead you to sin! Don't let anger control you or be fuel for revenge, not even for a day. 27.Don't give the slanderous accuser, the Devil, an opportunity to manipulate you!

TRUSTING IN GOD THAT OPENS DOORS

As it is written in Nehemiah 8:10 NIV, Do not grieve, for the joy of the Lord is your strength. You can have joy in challenging circumstances.

How, you ask? By leaning into what God is whispering to you. Do not surrender to fear in going forward. Stop permitting the fear of man from enabling you to walk in the destiny God has prepared for you. Fear and intimidation is a trap that holds you back. But when you place your confidence in the Lord, you will be seated in the high place. Proverbs 29:25 TPT.

Mostly, you will need to trust God from the bottom of your heart, in everything, for everything, from one step to the next. God knows your needs today and tomorrow, and the future, from the beginning of eternity, He is the author and finisher of your faith. "I am the Alpha and the Omega," says the Lord God, "who is, and who was, and who is to come, the Almighty." Revelation 1:8 NIV.

With that in mind, you don't need to figure everything out, because God has already answered your prayer requests, prophetically, according to his way, in His will, and in His time.

God is encouraging you to lean not on your own understanding. And neither is He expecting you to be co-dependent in receiving answers from humanity. You need to run to God's throne first and to seek His Kingdom before you run to the phone. Instead, turn to God. He is your comfort in your time of need.

TRUSTING IN GOD THAT OPENS DOORS

Trust God from the bottom of your heart;
don't try to figure out everything on your own.
Listen for God's voice in everything you do, everywhere you go;
he's the one who will keep you on track.
Don't assume that you know it all.
Run to God! Run from evil!
Your body will glow with health,
your very bones will vibrate with life!
Honor God with everything you own;
give him the first and the best.
Your barns will burst,
your wine vats will brim over.
But don't, dear friend, resent God's discipline;
don't sulk under his loving correction.
It's the child he loves that God corrects;
a father's delight is behind all this.
Proverbs 3:5-12 The Message

SCRIPTURE:
Hebrews 12:2 ESV
Looking to Jesus, the founder and perfecter of our faith, who for the
joy that was set before him endured the cross, despising the shame,
and is seated at the right hand of the throne of God.

PUSH THROUGH THIS

Expect the unexpected, in a good way, hold onto hope. Breakthrough and breaking out into your God-given destiny occur in God's time. Keep persevering. Keep praying. Keep pushing until something happens. Remain in God's peace.

Satan will attempt to dismantle your God-given purpose and destiny, using distractions. Recognise his cycle and cloning of lies, his purpose is to discourage, distract and tempt you to believe his lies. Do not surrender to him.

Build yourself up in the Lord, dig deep into His Word. One of Satan's subtle, yet suggestive strategies is to get you busy. Once you're busy, whatever that represents to you, he will exhaust you with thoughts that don't correspond with God's Truth, His Word.

The wrong voices will attempt to interrupt the flow and communication of God's Spirit with your spirit. Apply Godly discernment with each thought.

Busyness will keep you from reading God's Word. It will also attract exhaustion. Refrain from getting involved with other people's business which should be of no concern to you.

If you permit Satan to, he will keep you from attending church and attempt to steal your God-given peace and joy. You need to remain steadfast in God and to be calm and still, to tune into His still, small voice. His heavenly whisper. Close the door on Satan and every form of temptation, open your heart and spirit to God. Repent and turn away from all temptation.

PUSH THROUGH THIS

It is important you recognise Satan's schemes and tactics at its inception, nip them in the bud. It is time to take authority over the punishment Satan has been stinging you with.

He has attempted to convince you to recoil, for you to withdraw from society. Don't surrender to his pressure. You add value. In Christ you are more than a conqueror. You are a history maker. And a world changer.

You have been through enough. Keep your life simple. Stay away from what God's Spirit is whispering to you. Be attentive to God and His leading you and navigating your paths to safety and remain in His presence.

If you do not put God first, it is so easy to surrender to Satan's temptations. I do not worship Satan, however, you need to ask God early for discernment in every facet of your life, to be proactive in the Spirit realm.

Push through, your miracle is closer than you think. You are a breath and a heartbeat away from a miracle, through Divine deliverance.

SCRIPTURE:
2 Timothy 2:26 NIV
And that they will come to their senses and escape from the trap of the devil, who has taken them captive to do his will.

IN YOUR MIDNIGHT HOUR

Your thoughts have been pounding your mind. They have left you feeling restless and fatigued. An overactive, anxious mind works overtime during the day, resulting in sleepless nights. When you toss and turn, attempting to fall asleep, Satan magnifies the situation, producing tension in the atmosphere.

The mind is the battlefield, yet you have been persistent in prayer. Do not become weary in well doing. At times it appears you have experienced what feels like white knuckle syndrome and you're at the end of your rope, Jesus is your hope. He is the anchor of your soul.

I encourage you to persist in your walk on water faith and do not sink into despair. Hope = Healing Of Painful Emotions. Be encouraged, your time of deliverance is nigh. Get ready, get ready, get ready. Go for a walk, to refresh your soul. Speak to God during your walks. Perhaps, you can invite a friend to accompany you.

Be at peace. Remain hopeful and be encouraged. Today, explore new territories, experience exciting adventures, and appreciate every moment as momentous, and every minute which is miraculous. Expect and experience the exceptional, that represents Christ, today, and always.

SCRIPTURE:
Zechariah 9:12 NLT
Come back to the place of safety, all you prisoners who still have hope! I promise this very day that I will repay two blessings for each of your troubles.

HOLY SPIRIT BREATH

The words you speak will attract life or death in your present/future. When you speak and declare faith into a circumstance, speaking God's Word, God's Spirit will release life and transformation into what is refusing to budge.

If you walk in agreement with negativity, whatever life looks like for you at present, the results will be negative, it's an obvious statement. It is sometimes easier to stoke a fire of negativity, (rather than a posture of hope), which stirs up drama, pouting and an exaggerated performance, when you choose not to walk in agreement with what God is asking you to do.

Proverbs 18:21 AMP, Death and life are in the power of the tongue, and those who love it and indulge it will eat its fruit and bear the consequences of their words.

Alternatively, if you refuse to surrender to the pressure of defeat, or to give up on God's promises, it's a win-win situation. God will transform your life little by little, from glory to glory, where, in Christ you will live from God's authority and your circumstances will not have control over you.

As you transition through each situation that is turbulent, God's peace within you will calm the waters. But your words and attitude need to come into alignment with God's Word.

HOLY SPIRIT BREATH

You will come out sharper, stronger, wiser, humbler with increased compassion, when you surrender your will to God's will. When you speak His Word into your situation which appears impossible, wait with hope and expectancy as to what God's Holy Spirit will do. Observe how He will move, which will transform your life. In Christ, you will never be the same again.

Prophesy to the dry bones in your life. Whatever you are experiencing that is 'parched', speak the Word of God over it. Soak your soul and spirit in God's Word. There is life and death in your words, it is your choice to speak life and not to walk, and to speak in agreement with Satan.

Dismantle distractions which are the devil's intention to set you up, to get you upset. As Jesus responded to Satan when he attempted to tempt Jesus, Jesus responded, applying God's Word, by speaking, "It is written, Satan."

With God's help, identify early the 'trigger' mechanisms that set off your emotions that steal God's peace and joy in your life. Uproot bitterness, resentment and unforgiveness by not permitting those toxic thoughts to gain entry into your mind.

SCRIPTURE:
Ezekiel 37:9-10 NIV
9.Then he said to me, "Prophesy to the breath; prophesy, son of man, and say to it, 'This is what the Sovereign Lord says: Come, breath, from the four winds and breathe into these slain, that they may live.'" 10.So I prophesied as he commanded me, and breath entered them; they came to life and stood up on their feet-a vast army.

YOU ARE A NEW CREATION IN CHRIST

Your best years are yet ahead of you. Choose to live from victory. Jesus has already accomplished everything on the cross. The things of the past are simply that, let them go.

Do not permit your past to attempt to frame your present/future. Also, resist clinging to the things that God is finished with. Whatever that looks like to you.

Because when the season for that specific 'thing' is over in your life, if you attempt to extend its used by date, you will experience a struggle, as God's anointing is no longer working through you to advance in that direction. Naturally for each person, the specifics in your life involve your choices. Think new things. Stimulate your senses with beauty that inspires you to accomplish more, in a relaxed frame of mind.

Choose to enjoy everyday life, irrespective of how mundane some things may be to work through. It's your attitude which determines your altitude. With respect, so much of life is uneventful, but humanity cannot live for the highs, without encountering the valley experiences, that is the place where you grow in Christ, at an exponential pace.

Life advances at an alarming rate. Let go of everything that is occupying your mind that is attempting to dismantle what God has planned for you.

For some, the journey has been challenging for a while. Rest and relax. Recover and discover. Inhale inspiration. Exhale forgiveness.

YOU ARE A NEW CREATION IN CHRIST

2 Corinthians 4:8-11, ESV, 8. We are afflicted in every way, but not crushed; perplexed, but not driven to despair, 9.persecuted, but not forsaken, struck down, but not destroyed; 10.always carrying in the body the death of Jesus, so that the life of Jesus may also be manifested in our bodies. 11.For we who live are always being given over to death for Jesus' sake, so that the life of Jesus also may be manifested in our mortal flesh.

Step out from the shadows Ignited in inspiration. Resist distractions and procrastination. Prepare, plan, and pursue the path of your God-given destiny. Develop your voice. Live on purpose for a purpose. Be original. Your former mindsets have been nailed to the cross. Think new, fresh, creative thoughts and renew your mind with the Word of God.

Romans 12:2 AMP, And do not be conformed to this world [any longer with its superficial values and customs] but be transformed *and* progressively changed [as you mature spiritually] by the renewing of your mind [focusing on godly values and ethical attitudes], so that you may prove [for yourselves] what the will of God is, that which is good and acceptable and perfect [in His plan and purpose for you].

SCRIPTURE:
2 Corinthians 5:17 ESV
Therefore, if anyone is in Christ, he is a new creation. The old has passed away; behold, the new has come.

KEEP YOUR GAZE ON JESUS

Here, I share a moment in time regarding God's gift to me, photography. I hope my testimony will uplift your hope and faith in God.

Due to the low tide, there was a puddle of water in front of me, which was insufficient to capture reflections. God saturated the sky and the water in the distance, with His indescribable light. I looked ahead and quickly made my way to where the water was in abundance.

My message to you is no matter what situation you're in, God is right in it with you. Resist panic and overwhelm, keep your gaze on Jesus. Whether your challenges are due to your health, a lack in your finances, and/or relationships, He has already prepared your healing, or that of a loved one.

God is the supplier of all your needs. He restores the years the locusts have eaten. All things are possible with God, only believe. Shalom. Trust in Him for a miraculous outcome. Praise Him. The little you have, give to God and He will multiply it. Stay in faith.

SCRIPTURE:
Psalm 34:5 TPT
Gaze upon Him, join your life with his, and joy will come. Your faces will glisten with glory. You'll never wear that shame-face again.

Celebrate who you were created to be. Spontaneity and serendipity are freedom in the Spirit to make the right choices, to let go of your past, to forgive, and to strengthen your faith. Also to move at the right time, with the right people and to the right place.

Serendipity. Travelling along your God-given destination involves some tight corners, potholes, and unexpected turns. But it's worth it. Keep on going. There is no looking back.

Trusting God's faithfulness is knowing that He has prepared a way of escape for you. That doesn't mean you won't experience turbulence and trials, but God has equipped you to go through the fire and the water, and to come out on the other side victoriously, in Christ.

He has His hands over your life. Put your hand in His hand. This too shall pass. Where you are today, you won't remain. God is moving you and training you to go way over and beyond what you could ever imagine.

SCRIPTURE:
1 Corinthians 10:13 AMP
No temptation [regardless of its source] has overtaken or enticed you that is not common to human experience [nor is any temptation unusual or beyond human resistance]; but God is faithful [to His word- He is compassionate and trustworthy], and He will not let you be tempted beyond your ability [to resist], but along with the temptation He [has in the past and is now and] will [always] provide the way out as well, so that you will be able to endure it [without yielding, and will overcome temptation with joy].

IN THE HEAT OF THE BATTLE

When the heat of the battle is turned up, be rest assured that God is your source, your refuge. But seek first his kingdom and his righteousness, and all these things will be given to you as well. Matthew 6:33 NIV.

Turn to God, confide your feelings and fears to Him, He already knows the situation you are in. Draw into His presence in increased intimacy and receive His peace. Ask God for strategies for the battle you are in. A war comprises of different battles, with specific strategies. God will impart them to you. Listen with intentionality to His soft whisper. Be calm.

God's Word is His Spiritual prescription for your soul. Distance yourself from chatter and distractions and apply Godly wisdom with regards to who you confide your circumstances to.

Confidantes are rare. They comprise a handful of people you can truly trust, who will not leak your private life to the world. God is our refuge and strength, an ever-present help in trouble. Psalm 46:1 NIV.

Accessibility. Are you choosing to turn your back on new opportunities? Perhaps you're being influenced by other people's opinions. Resist being reduced by their limited thinking. Determine your Divine destiny by silencing the critics.

IN THE HEAT OF THE BATTLE

This is a new day, rise to new heights. Occupy your Divine purpose and inheritance by speaking God's Word and believing in His promises for your life. Religion is dry, parched, and lifeless, soak your soul and your spirit in God's Word and in His presence. There is no time like the present, it's a gift from God.

Every day I used to live petrified, but now I live in my God-given destiny. I live on purpose for a purpose, I am free to be me. And it's the same with you, or anyone else, what God anoints you to do and to become, is for His glory, which is indescribable. Your story for His glory.

I would not be able to tell my stories of survival and keeping my mind and head above the water to survive, sometimes experiencing acute, desperate moments. But, by God's grace, He has enabled me to live victoriously, and to become, in Him, that which is miraculous. And I'm not alone. God is no respecter of persons; He will do the same for you. Trust Him.

Your life experiences weave a miraculous, indestructible thread of hope, for humanity. Burst out of the staleness of your past, into the newness that God has already prepared for you. Be at peace. Be encouraged. Be you.

SCRIPTURE:
Daniel 3:24 NIV
Then King Nebuchadnezzar leaped to his feet in amazement and asked his advisers, "Weren't there three men that we tied up and threw into the fire?"

MOVE OUT FROM THE SHADOWS

This day is like no other. Expect the unexpected, in a good way, walk with your head held high, your chest out and your shoulders back. Believe in God and not in your past, nor what others say about you. Stop giving Satan power over your life in believing his lies.

Re-shape and transform your thinking with studying and applying God's Word. Do not conform to the pattern of this world but be transformed by the renewing of your mind. Then you will be able to test and approve what God's will is-his good, pleasing, and perfect will. Romans 12:2 NIV.

Christ in you, attracts the authority of heaven. There is so much power in those words. Whatever is coming against you, knowing deep down in your soul and spirit, that your identity is in Christ Jesus, and not in the things of this world, you have nothing to dread or to fear.

Instead, you can go forward with the courage and the boldness of a lion. No man shall be able to stand before you all the days of your life. Just as I was with Moses, so I will be with you. I will not leave you or forsake you. Joshua 1:5 ESV.

Travel through this day, not in your strength, but in the power and authority of God. Deliberately step out in faith and do what God has already accomplished for you supernaturally, in your present/future. This day represents history to God.

MOVE OUT FROM THE SHADOWS

Repel fear, the presence of God is enabling you to conquer and to dismantle every obstacle, in the mighty Name of Jesus. Recline in His peace, every little thing is going to be okay.

9.For this reason also [because He obeyed and so completely humbled Himself], God has highly exalted Him and bestowed on Him the name which is above every name, 10.so that at the name of Jesus every knee shall bow [in submission], of those who are in heaven and on earth and under the earth, 11.and that every tongue will confess *and* openly acknowledge that Jesus Christ is Lord (sovereign God), to the glory of God the Father. Philippians 2:9-11 AMP.

SCRIPTURE:
Romans 8:28 NLT
And we know that God causes everything to work together for the good of those who love God and are called according to his purpose for them.

WHEN YOU ARE FEELING DESPERATE

Are you feeling overwhelmed with the pressures of life? Are the people around you attempting to control you? Or are you experiencing moments of panic, hopelessness and feeling so desperate you don't know what to do?

When trials and tribulations are on the increase, from experience, my advice is to separate yourself, not to isolate yourself from society, but to come away and to be with God the Father.

Collect your thoughts. What takes priority when you have a list of 'urgent' things to do, or people to attend to? In what area have you become overcommitted in wanting to please people?

It's a fact, some individuals will never be completely satisfied. Stop, from this moment attempting to expect somebody to change, or to appreciate you, whether it be family or friends.

Sometimes control and manipulation is used as leverage to bring change. But it never works. And it leaves you feeling frustrated, unfulfilled, and rejected. Thinking toxic thoughts, affects you. It upsets you, whilst the people you are angry at, are out having a good time, unaware of your emotions. Let it go. And let God.

Only God can change the people closest to you. And, more importantly, pray to God to change you, for Him to help you and to heal your inner soul, and to view your circumstances from His perspective. You will experience acceptance, release, and His peace.

Mental and emotional exhaustion almost takes you to the edge. Before you arrive at that point, I recommend you evaluate the situation for what it is. Keep your gaze on Jesus.

WHEN YOU ARE FEELING DESPERATE

Refrain from making complex circumstances bigger than what they are, by thinking and speaking words of negativity, irrespective of how dire your current situation may be. Apply Godly wisdom and walk away, if necessary, to avoid tension and enmity.

Careless conversations carry consequences. Life is precious. It is short. And it is fragile, don't waste time and energy on distractions and words spoken in anger, that cannot be retracted.

Some things need to be dealt with, with God's help, speaking the truth in love as it is written in Ephesians 4:15 NIV, Instead, speaking the truth in love, we will grow to become in every respect the mature body of him who is the head, that is, Christ.

I also encourage you to journal your feelings to God. It will give you an opportunity to express yourself in writing to Him, which is cathartic. Be still before God and listen for his quiet whisper.

What do you need to surrender to God, to be set free? Only you can answer that. Let God take your load and burdens, as Jesus died on the cross for humanity, your sins in exchange for His healing touch, which you need. Jesus redeemed humanity from hopelessness to build faith and hope in His children, for life.

God is in control when your circumstances appear to be out of control. God is the God of the impossible. Only believe. Stand up, stand out, stand strong. Remaining standing. Jesus, You are the Prince of Peace, in the centre of the storm, and always.

In closing, you need a 'breather', a break from the pressures of life. Something must give. Otherwise, you could crack under the unrealistic expectations you're experiencing.

Learn to listen to what your heart is saying to you. Draw boundary lines. Deal with the issues that are pressing in on you. Count your blessings daily. Breathe easy, every little thing is going to be okay. Learn to say no without feeling guilty, it becomes easier with time.

SCRIPTURE:
Colossians 3:15 ESV
And let the peace of Christ rule in your hearts, to which indeed you were called in one body. And be thankful.

GOD IS YOUR BODYGUARD

Never give up. Nor give in when the battle is on. Stand and keep on standing. Even if your progress is one inch at a time, you're doing well. You're an overcomer, a champion and more than a conqueror, in Christ.

You have not come this far to quit. As a born-again believer in Christ, you have the resurrection power of Jesus Christ residing in you. Don't back down or be intimidated by the lies and deception of Satan.

For some, you're exhausted from the fight, I urge you to lean in and draw your strength from God. You're too close to breakthrough and victory, to walk away now. I know you will keep moving forward even though every fibre in your being is stretched to the limit, keep your gaze on Jesus. All things are possible, only believe.

During my photo shoot recently, Satan threw everything at me to prevent me from capturing a sunrise that God had called me to. I would not surrender, but in the heat of the battle I asked God for His strategies.

God overruled what the devil thought he could use to defeat me and have me whimpering and angry and frustrated, but, before each shoot, I dedicate each shoot to God. Yes, I did get a big splash and shouted out to Jesus because I was in deep water and so was my equipment, and He rescued me. He will do the same for you, irrespective of your circumstance. Shalom. Shabbat. Be encouraged.

SCRIPTURE:
Psalm 34:20 TPT
God will be your bodyguard to protect you when trouble is near. Not one bone will be broken.

WHEN YOU ARE WEAK, GOD IS YOUR STRENGTH

It is exhilarating knowing that God pulverises the plans of the enemy as you surrender everything to Him.

God's Word has all the answers you will ever need. Rise above your circumstances and move beyond them by placing your trust in God. Distract the detractor by thinking and meditating on good things. And now, dear brothers and sisters, one final thing. Fix your thoughts on what is true, and honorable, and right, and pure, and lovely, and admirable. Think about things that are excellent and worthy of praise. Philippians 4:8 NLT.

Break the barrier of fear and shatter the lies of the devil by walking and believing in the promises of God. God is with you. He is for you, in every situation. And He is working through you and strengthening you. Shalom.

Beat your ploughshares into swords and your pruning hooks into spears; let the weak say, "I am strong!" Joel 3:10 AMP. As a thermostat, sets the atmosphere, so do you, in Christ.

SCRIPTURE:
2 Corinthians 12:9 AMP
But He has said to me, "My grace is sufficient for you [My lovingkindness and My mercy are more than enough-always available-regardless of the situation]; for [My] power is being perfected [and is completed and shows itself most effectively] in [your] weakness." Therefore, I will all the more gladly boast in my weaknesses, so that the power of Christ [may completely enfold me and] may dwell in me.

BE IN THE RHYTHM OF GOD'S HEARTBEAT

You are not alone. Not now. Never. God is with you. He is protecting you. His angels are around you.

God is wrapping and enfolding you in His blanket of love. In Christ, you have nothing to fear. Fear is False Evidence Appearing Real. Anxiety is a breeding ground from Satan in believing his lies. That has to stop. Anxiety is layered with uncertainty, expecting the worst outcome, which also attracts dread.

Satan will lie to you about what you are going through, whether it involves your child or children, your spouse, or anything else that is relevant in your life. If you grew up in financial lack, Satan attempts to convince you that your finances, and your future will always be in short supply. When you have exhausted yourself from overthinking your situation, you start speaking words of anxiety, dread, and fear.

If you have lived that lie, particularly associated with finances, break off Satan's attempt to derail your faith by believing in God for your breakthrough. How? By taking authority over Satan and speaking God's Word as I have written previously.

List Scriptures involved with walking away from your old mindsets of never being enough or never having enough, whether that be associated with your finances, your health, or in relationships, immerse your soul in scriptures that relate to victory, breakthrough, and abundance, in Christ.

Stop reciting what you have spoken over your life and that of your family. Push back those invitations from the devil to lie awake at night and to dread the next day. Saturate your soul and spirit with God's Truth, His Word. His Truth releases revelation and freedom in Christ.

BE IN THE RHYTHM OF GOD'S HEARTBEAT

Thread your story and testimony with hope, woven with the love of God, into a beautiful tapestry, decreeing something good is going to happen to you and to your family. With each breath, thank God for your life and for your loved ones.

His hand is upon you and your family. Release your faith in God and experience the loosening of the grip of fear and anxiety from you, as God's peace flows through you. Guilt and shame tend to isolate you. Stop it. Only God can heal you and bring you out victorious, in Christ. Shalom.

SCRIPTURE:
Colossians 2:2 TPT
I am contending for you that your hearts will be wrapped in the comfort of heaven and woven together into love's fabric. This will give you access to all the riches of God as you experience the revelation of God's great mystery-Christ.

PUT GOD FIRST

It's in the little things that can bring you the most pleasure. Although the Koropuku falls, South Island, New Zealand, weren't the biggest, or the most popular falls, due to their size and location, however, I most certainly enjoyed the tranquillity of those falls. The effort involved walking to them was worth it.

Sometimes, in fact, often, the best things in life, if they are not free, neither are they the most expensive. Perhaps humanity places too much emphasis and value on the supposedly sought after things that we think we 'have to have' to make us 'happy' and content, instead of seeing how we can serve others, as well as enjoying down time to refresh and to replenish our souls.

In the past, I have been influenced by the airwaves that have been bombarded by what society and the media 'insist' on you acquiring something to make you happy, by using slogans such as, 'you deserve it'. That's control and manipulation because true joy can only come from the Spirit of God.

It's okay to have things, as long as they don't have you and me. God gives His children the desires of their hearts, but materialism is idolatry. 'Things' should not control you or me, competing for our First Love, God.

SCRIPTURE:
Psalm 37:4 ESV
Delight yourself in the Lord, and he will give you the desires of your heart.

LIVE IN THE MOMENT

Here I share a moment in time regarding God's gift to me, photography. I hope my testimony will uplift your hope and faith in God. Recently I stood on the rock shelf at Snapper Rocks. It's not for the timid of heart standing and watching the big waves accelerate towards me, but it is thrilling.

But the difference between foolishness and Godly wisdom is being intentional regarding each step that you make and take. You need to hear from God before you make fleshy decisions that could have catastrophic results.

As much as I thrive on the big waves in capturing God's power, I also stand in reverential awe of God and His power. I spend a generous amount of time in researching the conditions for each beach or location where God intends for me to shoot at.

Also, before each shoot, I dedicate the shoot to God, and I listen to Him as to where I should stand. A foot outside of God's suggested space and I know I'm in trouble. But, within His perimeter of safety, I've had big waves and sea spray around me, without touching myself or my equipment.

Today, I urge you not to make decisions without waiting upon the Lord and hearing and being obedient to His soft whisper. Be safe. Be still. Be adaptable in Christ.

SCRIPTURE:
Hebrews 11:6 NLT
And it is impossible to please God without faith. Anyone who wants to come to him must believe that God exists and that he rewards those who sincerely seek him.

YOU ADD VALUE

Have you hit a pothole in the road, where you are experiencing delays in your God-given destiny which is causing you to be frustrated?

It is so easy to become discouraged, disgruntled and to be influenced by your feelings to give up, as the journey is too difficult and its taking too long to reach your destination, when you experience delays and detours.

This is the time to persevere, God has created you for a time such as this. One of the tricks that Satan uses is for you to look at other people's lives on social media and to become discouraged as you have a longing for your life to measure up to their life. Apart from what it takes to get where they are at, are they fulfilled? And, besides, their life isn't perfect.

Competition and glancing at someone else's life journey on social media, not only side-tracks you, but you don't know what is going on in their life. When your attention is attracted to their so-called perfect lifestyle, and you scroll through their posts, which are perfectly edited to impress and to draw attention; that is when vulnerability makes its presence felt, usually in the form of jealousy and envy. Initially manifested as a trickle, then as a flood, if your emotions are not curtailed.

You need to make a healthy choice regarding occupying yourself with activities that draw your attention into something new and fresh, and to keep God in first place.

SCRIPTURE:
2 Timothy 3:16-17 NIV
16.All Scripture is God-breathed and is useful for teaching, rebuking, correcting and training in righteousness, 17.so that the servant of God may be thoroughly equipped for every good work.

WHAT ARE YOU WAITING FOR?

Have you hit a pothole in the road, where you are experiencing delays in your God-given destiny which is causing you to be frustrated?

It is so easy to become discouraged, disgruntled and to be influenced by your feelings to give up, as the journey is too difficult and its taking too long to reach your destination, when you experience delays and detours.

This is the time to persevere, God has created you for a time such as this. One of the tricks that Satan uses is for you to look at other people's lives on social media and to become discouraged as you have a longing for your life to measure up to their life. Apart from what it takes to get where they are at, are they fulfilled? And, besides, their life isn't perfect.

Competition and glancing at someone else's life journey on social media, not only side-tracks you, but you don't know what is going on in their life.

When your attention is attracted to their so-called perfect lifestyle, and you scroll through their posts, which are perfectly edited to impress and to draw attention; that is when vulnerability makes its presence felt, usually in the form of jealousy and envy. Initially manifested as a trickle, then as a flood, if your emotions are not curtailed.

You need to make a healthy choice regarding occupying yourself with activities that draw your attention into something new and fresh, and to keep God in first place.

WHAT ARE YOU WAITING FOR?

When you experience, what seems like constant setbacks, and you sense you're not making any progress, or if you are, it's not in big strides. It's in that moment, when you're feeling vulnerable that you need to be aware of remaining silent and not speaking careless words. And to guard your heart.

Nothing comes from cursing or complaining, but, cursing when facing challenges, opens the door wide for Satan to manifest himself in your situation. Sometimes, the delays in your progress are originated by God in using setbacks, to take you to another level, for a comeback.

God knows the importance of you being transformed by the renewing of your mind, as it is written in Romans 12:2. Promotion in the spirit comes from a succession of tests, and your attitude towards them. Embrace the challenges, not in your own strength, but, with God's help.

Be encouraged in the middle of a sticky place. Ask God for suggestions, strategies, and solutions to move you through to the other side, live from a place of victory. You will come out wiser, stronger and God will use you to encourage people around you who are stuck. You can do this, with God's help. Be at peace. The title for this message is related to procrastination. It is time to make a move, in Godly wisdom.

SCRIPTURE:
Psalm 37:7 TPT
Quiet your heart in his presence and wait patiently for Yahweh. And don't think for a moment that the wicked, in their prosperity, are better off than you.

NO ONE CAN HOLD YOU BACK

Here I share a moment in time regarding God's gift to me, photography. I hope my testimony will uplift your hope and faith in God.

Recently, during my photo shoot, whilst sitting safely on the concrete wall at Snapper Rocks, I witnessed the surge of God's power, and the acceleration of those powerful waves crashing against the wall below my feet. God reminded me, yet again, He has your situation in His hands.

I urge you to hold onto hope. Resist walking in agreement with the whispering lies from Satan. Speak God's Word to the devil, by informing him, as Jesus did, "It is written."

You need to take every thought captive to the obedience of Jesus Christ. *We are* destroying sophisticated arguments and every exalted *and* proud thing that sets itself up against the [true] knowledge of God, and *we are* taking every thought *and* purpose captive to the obedience of Christ. 2 Corinthians 10:5 AMP. You are not alone. Shalom.

God encourages you to cast your cares on Him, casting all your anxieties on him, because he cares for you. 1 Peter 5:7 ESV. Be sober-minded; be watchful. Your adversary the devil prowls around like a roaring lion, seeking someone to devour. 1 Peter 5:8 ESV.

Submit yourselves therefore to God. Resist the devil, and he will flee from you, James 4:7 ESV.

NO ONE CAN HOLD YOU BACK

The battle belongs to the Lord. But at the same time, it is important to obey God in what He is speaking to your heart. God wants you to rest in His peace, and yet, to co-operate with Him in faith, which is trusting in God for a good outcome. Our faith needs to be activated in what God has already accomplished today, as today is history for Him.

Sitting on that concrete wall at Snapper Rocks, spoke volumes to me as I was safe irrespective of how the ocean was raging around me.

Do not do life alone, you become vulnerable to Satan. You are created for community. And, in Christ, you are more than a conqueror. I do not worship, or fear Satan, but you need to be reminded of the authority you have in Christ, as a born-again believer, which is to rise above what you are going through, with God's help, as you are seated in heavenly places, in and with Christ Jesus.

SCRIPTURE:
Isaiah 60:1 AMP
"Arise [from spiritual depression to a new life], shine [be radiant with the glory *and* brilliance of the Lord]; for your light has come, and the glory *and* brilliance of the Lord has risen upon you."

PURPOSE WITH A PASSION

After years of searching for what was at my fingertips, to ease the pain of my past, I was given a camera for my Birthday. It was more than a gift. It was a navigational tool that God has used to heal me from years of living depressed.

It was God's purpose to use my camera as direction to His Light and His Truth, and His Word. Depression was not and is not my identity. My identity is in Christ Jesus, and so is yours.

Jesus rescued me from the brink of despair and a longing to be 'normal' like everyone else around me. Whatever normal represented. Humanity judges the exterior for the interior. Never judge a book by its cover as the saying goes.

God looks at our heart and not at the outward appearance, as it is written God's Word. But the Lord said to Samuel, "Do not consider his appearance or his height, for I have rejected him. The Lord does not look at the things people look at. People look at the outward appearance, but the Lord looks at the heart.", 1 Samuel 16:7 NIV

I always felt less than, inferior and inadequate. Different because of experiencing serotonin imbalance issues from the age of twelve, which was a turning point in my life.

Stress, yes, at such a young age, was a trigger mechanism, coupled with the cusp of entering my teenage years, where hormones played an active role, combined with the serotonin imbalance.

PURPOSE WITH A PASSION

When I was growing up, depression and anxiety were not discussed in public, not even amongst family members. I lived a life of hell regarding the turmoil in my mind. There was no suggestion of visiting a clinical psychologist, as no one knew what I was experiencing.

I have noticed in recent years the use of 'labelling' humanity with specifics related to mental illness, or mental wellbeing. I am strongly convinced that everyone needs to be sensitive regarding 'slapping' labels on society, of any age, particularly when you are closely associated with that person. Words hurt and they cannot be retracted, besides, their impact is lasting.

Yes, I have heard and read of instances where individuals did not know who they were labelling. Perhaps they knew that person from a distance, perse.

I write about living from victory, in Christ, as that is who I have become, victorious in Christ. My passion for God's children runs deep, to reach out to the hurting, who are experiencing rejection and abandonment. Or else to express love in words, a hug, or simply to listen intently to the other person, that is what makes my heartbeat for humanity.

The passion God has birthed deep within my soul is to bring joy to everyone I come into contact with, with words that resonate in the souls of humanity. It was at that moment of reaching out, I lost sight of grief that gripped my heart for decades.

PURPOSE WITH A PASSION

God enables me to extend myself to the lost, the lonely, and the broken-hearted. God's gifts are His purpose to loosen that grip and to release flight to the dreams that become a reality. I live on purpose for a purpose, for a common cause, to the audience of One and to be the hands, eyes, ears, voice, and feet of Jesus Christ.

Messages written in this book are intended to stir the embers within you, into flames of enthusiasm, galvanised by faith. Shalom. You are not a mistake; you are God's masterpiece.

Occupy, possess, inhabit your God-given destiny. Darkness and everything that attempts to hide in it, surrenders to the Light and Truth of Jesus Christ.

Faith and hope in God is the runway to your dreams. The Holy Spirit is the wind beneath your wings. He enables you to rise above the opposing forces and navigates you safely to your destiny. Trust Him. Rejoice in Him.

SCRIPTURE:
Ephesians 3:20 TPT
Never doubt God's mighty power to work in you and accomplish all this. He will achieve infinitely more than your greatest request, your most unbelievable dream, and exceed your wildest imagination! He will outdo them all, for his miraculous power constantly energizes you.

YOU WILL GET THROUGH THIS

You and I don't know what is around the corner, but God does, and that is a good thing, particularly when your life journey is involved with loss.

Grief and mourning are, of course, associated with loss, particularly the loss of a loved one. The process of saying goodbye to the one you are losing due to illness, or have just lost, is never easy, whether they are young or mature, or their illness has been lengthy or short. There is always trauma involved, a numbness settles deep within your soul, and that takes time to ease and subside.

No one can prepare you for such loss. Grief and mourning don't have a time frame. It is insensitive to inform someone to get over their emotions regarding their sadness and loss, whilst their grief and pain is still raw.

Grief and sadness are manifested in various forms, it can also represent the loss of a job or having to sell a home due to foreclosure, a divorce, or a loss in a relationship.

Experiencing grief and mourning is natural, and so is releasing your emotions through tears. It is unhealthy to stifle your emotions and to pretend you have everything together. God created tears for that purpose. A release.

Each day is a challenge when you are grieving. I'm being transparent in acknowledging the truth, but with that challenge, God is with you, in you and for you, working healing each day as you surrender your grief to Him.

YOU WILL GET THOUGH THIS

Sometimes, the grief is too deep to talk about. You simply want someone to be there, without saying much. Surround yourself with people you know you can trust and who are compassionate, and, at the same time, they will encourage you to move forward at your pace.

Those close to you, because they love you, will challenge you, when to go out and to meet new people, to visit new places. Sometimes, when you are experiencing grief, your proclivity is to wind back the clock and re-visit places associated with the past. It is nostalgic.

I'm not suggesting that is not a good thing, but it may be wounding to return to some places too soon, that are poignant and represent strong memories. My suggestion would be to give it time before returning to locations that evoke emotions.

As you have read and heard the expression, there is a silver lining to each cloud. And the clouds of desperation will lift as you quietly look for the bright things in each day. Counting your blessings daily, as you gather your strength. God has created you on purpose for a purpose.

What is in your hands that you can use to bless someone else? At the right time, when your strength is returning, it's wise to move one step at a time, in going forward, to reach out and connect with new people in new places.

It is normally in the middle of your pain and loss, that you ask God questions, some of which remain unanswered. And sometimes the questions are asked from an angry, broken, and a desperate heart. God knows your pain. But that does not mean that He is insensitive and far removed from you.

YOU WILL GET THROUGH THIS

You possess tremendous strength and courage; in Christ, you are stronger in your faith than you realise. With the passage of time, you will reflect and look back on how far God has brought you in the process of healing your pain.

Again, give yourself time to heal through your grief. You will laugh again. You will arise again. Be good to yourself. Be patient. Be at peace. But do not hide in your pain. 1.There is a season (a time appointed) for everything and a time for every delight *and* event *or* purpose under heaven— 2.A time to be born and a time to die; A time to plant and a time to uproot what is planted. Ecclesiastes 3:1-2 AMP.

SCRIPTURE:
Revelation 21:4 NLT
He will wipe away every tear from their eyes, and there will be no more death or sorrow or crying or pain. All these things are gone forever.

ONWARDS AND UPWARDS

Here I share a moment in time regarding God's gift to me, photography. I hope my testimony will uplift your hope and faith in God. The mountains are a place of rest for me. How about you, where do you spend your time resting in the Lord?

Nothing comes from wishing or dreaming, you need to take it one step further and galvanise your faith in God by partnering with Him in taking one step of faith at a time, in your day to day living. Keep your eyes on God, whilst resisting Satan's deception.

I have completed several shoots at Crown Range Road, New Zealand, which overlooks Roaring Meg and the back of the Remarkables mountain range, Queenstown, which represents heaven on earth to me.

To reach this location it is (usually) on icy roads, whilst it's freezing cold, with snowy conditions. But the sacrifice is worth it. I normally grip my steering wheel tight when driving in those icy weather conditions.

Whatever is opposing you at present, it will not be permanent. God is in you. He is with you. God is for you. God put on my heart to encourage you, particularly if you have your back against the wall in a 'tight' situation. God has made a way out for you. Trust Him.

In Christ, you will more than weather the storm and learn to live above your circumstances by taking authority over Satan, as you apply God's Word, and being led by His Spirit.

ONWARDS AND UPWARDS

With time, you will come out stronger, wiser, more compassionate, and live from a place of humility. God is an incredible Teacher. He uses life to sharpen and shape you, and to develop character deep within you, which enables you to go through each battle from a posture of faith and hope in God, and to live from His victory.

Forgiveness will become a way of life for you when you drop all offences. Now the Lord is the Spirit, and where the Spirit of the Lord is, there is freedom, 2 Corinthians 3:17 NIV. In completion, the morning of this shoot was like every other one I'd been on before at Crown Range Road.

I was layered with so much clothing I could barely move. I stepped over the style and made my way up the steep hill, which is rugged terrain I'm so familiar with. A biting southerly wind pierced through layers of my clothing, but it was like coming home.

All to see my Creator, Who was about to paint the sky in His glorious colours. The effort you put in, is the outcome of blessings God will shower upon you in your life. Blessed to be a blessing. Peace be still.

SCRIPTURE:
2 Chronicles 20:17 ESV
'You will not need to fight in this battle. Stand firm, hold your position, and see the salvation of the Lord on your behalf, O Judah, and Jerusalem.' "Do not be afraid and do not be dismayed. Tomorrow go out against them, and the Lord will be with you."

DEVELOPED IN THE LIGHT

All things bright and beautiful, the Lord God made them all. In Christ, I celebrate light and brightness, as I spent too many years in the sombreness and darkness associated with my past. Besides, when you and I get to heaven, it is bright.

The Light of Christ repels the darkness, it exposes all lies, deception and anything that has been hidden, Jesus' Light and Truth have cancelled all the lies the devil lures you to believe.

You know your identity is in Christ, not in what people think or say about you. If you've been hiding because of pain, ask God to heal you, it's time to step up and step out and to gain momentum going forward and to strengthen your voice.

Stand up, stand out. Come out from the shadows and advance into your God-given destiny.

SCRIPTURE:
Isaiah 59:19 AMPC
So [as the result of the Messiah's intervention] they shall [reverently] fear the name of the Lord from the west, and His glory from the rising of the sun. When the enemy shall come in like a flood, the Spirit of the Lord will lift up a standard against him and put him to flight [for he will come like a rushing stream which the breath of the Lord drives].

RETRAIN YOUR THINKING

Occupy the reality of your God-given destiny by posturing yourself in the centre of God's will. Birds fly in V-formation as they 'share' the resistance of the wind.

You are anointed in Christ to fulfil your role, but you need to live balanced. It is important to encourage others to grow from the experience you have.

Burn out manifests itself when you have exhausted your God-given gifts by not taking time out. Breather breaks are essential. It's not easy letting go and letting God come into certain situations, particularly where you have excelled yourself, in Christ.

It's easier for you to accomplish much, instead of spending time and energy on equipping other people. You are not selfish, particularly with age, it is simply quicker to accomplish more from your experience, than to train and empower other people.

It is time to refresh and to recharge your batteries and to let go. Retrain your brain to work smarter, not harder. Prepare and train the future generations with the exceptional experience you possess.

Procrastination can set in. In this case, replace, 'if only' and 'but' with 'I choose to.' Whatever God has put in your hand, use it for His Glory.

SCRIPTURE:
Deuteronomy 20:4 NLT
'For the Lord your God is going with you! He will fight for you against your enemies, and he will give you victory!'

YOU ARE A HISTORY MAKER IN CHRIST

No matter what it takes, in Christ you can rise above fear, dread, anger, and anxiety, they are like the wind. Those 'feelings' disrupt and dismantle your peace, in Christ.

The tenancy of those 'residents' need to be evacuated from your mind and replaced with the Word and promises of God. The emotions associated with the spirit of fear, dread, anxiety, etcetera, which have occupied your thought life, for some, in fact, for far too long, and have attempted to influence and misalign your identity, in Christ Jesus, they cannot remain.

The feelings and emotions associated with fear, dread, and the like, have attempted to siphon your joy, in Christ, which is your strength. You cannot mix oil, the anointing of the Holy Spirit, with Satan's deadly lies, representing vinegar, with deadly emotions such as bitterness, resentment and unforgiveness.

It's a strategy of the devil to exhaust you. Keep your eyes and mind fixed on the Prince of Peace, Jesus. Be intentional. Be inspired. Become who God created you to be, by the renewal of your mind, Romans 12:2, and by studying His Word. You have what it takes to accomplish much, in Christ Jesus. You are more than a conqueror, Romans 8:28, and a champion in Christ. Stay the course. Run your race. Cross the finish line strong in the Lord. This is what He created you for. New beginnings.

SCRIPTURE:
Revelation 12:11 AMP
And they overcame *and* conquered him because of the blood of the Lamb and because of the word of their testimony, for they did not love their life *and* renounce their faith even when faced with death.

IT'S TIME FOR CHANGE

Sometimes you think your flesh is influencing your decisions, and, at times, it does, but, on other occasions, it is God speaking to your heart.

You know your season has ended, when your passion to continue with whatever you have been doing, runs dry. The creativity, or the thought processes involved, are no longer spontaneous. And your desire to be in that place of employment has dried up too.

It is time to think carefully and to be quiet before God. Seek His wisdom through His Word. Journal your thoughts and emotions regarding where you are at. Ponder your next step.

What does it look like? What will your new role involve, and at which company? It could be a complete change of what you are familiar with professionally.

Sometimes, you think you have made the right choice professionally, only to discover the shoe does not fit well. That is not a mistake, it's not too late to change the direction of your career.

You need to be professionally fulfilled. A large portion of your time is spent at work. The role needs to be stimulating and at the same time, it's important that you enjoy the people you work for, and with.

Perhaps a move will be involved. And maybe you need to research educational options to secure a position that is profitable and pleasurable, in every sense.

IT'S TIME FOR CHANGE

Sometimes God will put you, in what seems like a precarious position, where circumstances appear dire, which makes you feel desperate and out of your depth. Perhaps God is nudging you to take a leap of faith into the unknown, involving calculated risks. Staleness invites stagnation. Impulsiveness is costly.

There is no time for foolish decisions as they are costly. Think carefully before you leap, and at the same time, apply Godly wisdom.

Embrace the new challenges and change with an open heart and mind. When circumstances become stale, you know deep down within your heart and soul it is time to make a move, one way or the other. Be intentional. Be still.

SCRIPTURE:
Isaiah 43:19 TPT
I am doing something brand new, something unheard of. Even now it sprouts and grows and matures. Don't you perceive it? I will make a way in the wilderness and open up flowing streams in the desert.

FOOD FOR THOUGHT

Whilst on a photoshoot recently I waded on the peripheral of the ocean. The tide was coming in, the sand beneath my feet and tripod surrendered very quickly to the water.

God called me out to the deep, not too deep, but out from the shallow water amongst the rocks. The sand was stable, I was able to capture memorable shots and anticipate, with each wave, where I'd capture my next shot.

If I'd remained in the shallows, I wouldn't have had the opportunity to 'grow' as a photographer. Momentum replaces stagnancy. With God all things are possible, only believe.

Sometimes going out into the deep involves inconvenience, which could represent reaching out to someone who is in need. As much as you know they are needy, it could be exhaustion that speaks to your soul, almost convincing you why you are unable to assist that person or family, who require help.

It is not always easy to stretch yourself, you are not selfish. From personal experience, growth comes from total surrender to God's will in your life. God commands humanity to love our neighbour and to give them a cup of cold water.

Life has changed considerably since COVID. It has become a lot more complicated and people are more independent, insular, and lonely. Live life not for self, instead, reach out in kindness and compassion. You can't always appreciate or be aware of the pain in other people's lives.

FOOD FOR THOUGHT

Your smile and acts of kindness, not just words, could restore dignity and purpose in the lost, the lonely and the hurting.

Be kind. Be patient. Become compassionate. Greatness is always on the other side of inconvenience. You never know the time when you will be in need, and that is why good relationships are vital. We are created for community, and we need each other.

SCRIPTURE:

1 Corinthians 13:3-7 NIV

3.If I give all I possess to the poor and give over my body to hardship that I may boast, but do not have love, I gain nothing. 4.Love is patient, love is kind. It does not envy, it does not boast, it is not proud. 5.It does not dishonor others, it is not self-seeking, it is not easily angered, it keeps no record of wrongs. 6.Love does not delight in evil but rejoices with the truth. 7.It always protects, always trusts, always hopes, always perseveres.

THE TOOLS IN YOUR HAND

I honour God and my husband, Keith, for enabling me to stand strong during the years of depression that gripped my life, originating from loss, particularly from two miscarriages. As I have written previously, a camera, being God's purpose for my life, has changed the years of hopelessness and living without direction, to a life of purpose and fulfilment.

As a mature Fine Art Landscape Photographer, cracking my bedding during the early hours of the morning to go on photoshoots, gives me an appetite to help others see the light at the end of the tunnel. It is my God-given passion to equip and educate humanity who are experiencing opposition, and acute anxiety.

Maturity is a blessing as it has enabled me to gather strength and wisdom from God that will ease the burden other people may be experiencing. The photos I take are seen through God's lens and my purpose is to bring glory to God through His creation, and joy and peace to His people.

Jesus came to bring life to His children in abundance. It is God's purpose for all humanity to be His eyes, ears, hands, feet, and voice. Humanity attempted to silence me. Now I'm ready to roar to the world about Jesus Christ. What are you doing with your God-given tools in your hand?

SCRIPTURE:
Philippians 3:10-11 NLT
10.I want to know Christ and experience the mighty power that raised him from the dead. I want to suffer with him, sharing in his death, 11.so that one way or another I will experience the resurrection from the dead!

HEALING IN HOPE

Resist replaying the repetitive thoughts that are 'immersed' in regret. That mindset is unproductive and potentially harmful to your well-being.

Replace regrets, negativity, and hopelessness, which involve thinking in arrears, with thoughts that magnify God's promises for your life, it's time for you to move ahead. Refuse to live in the existence of your yesteryears. God created you on purpose for a purpose. Resist self-pity and pity parties, it's Satan's trick to tempt you to surrender to his lies. The Truth and Light are in Jesus Christ.

In Christ, you are gifted, talented and your best years are yet ahead of you. Gather threads of hope and weave a beautiful blanket woven with God's love. Reach out and embrace the hurting, with strong threads of forgiveness, hope, healing, love, laughter, and new beginnings.

With that blanket, extend a hand of hope to someone whom you can share it with. You are created for a time such as this to impact somebody else's life. God never intended for you to exist in loneliness and isolation. Shalom.

Burst out of the staleness associated with your past, into the newness that God has already prepared for you. Be at peace. Be encouraged. Be you.

SCRIPTURE:
Jeremiah 30:17 ESV
'For I will restore health to you, and your wounds I will heal, declares the Lord, because they have called you an outcast:' 'It is Zion, for whom no one cares!'

JOY COMES IN THE MORNING

Rejoice in today. Celebrate your victories, in and through Jesus Christ. Reach up. Reach out. See yourself as you are created, in Christ, victorious. Joy comes in the morning, particularly after a 'long' night of suffering.

Stop justifying being 'you', in an attempt for approval. Define your boundaries, but do not build walls, establish honour, value, and respect. Perhaps you have been downtrodden for too long.

People will regard you, the way you see yourself. Your identity is not in other people's opinions of you, neither is it in your history. Instead, it is in Jesus Christ.

Stop permitting your poisonous past to 'haemorrhage' your progress in moving forward, resulting from the quagmire of your thinking associated with defeat.

Ask God to heal you. Receive your healing from Him. Trust God. Proclaim a fresh start, with transformational mindsets, and transition into new territory with dignity and courage.

Get up. Get out. Get moving. Time waits for no one. Stop procrastinating. You can do all things through Christ Who strengthens you. Shalom. Live amazed today at Who God is.

SCRIPTURE:
Psalm 30:4-5 NLT
4.Sing to the Lord, all you godly ones! Praise his holy name. 5.For his anger lasts only a moment, but his favor lasts a lifetime! Weeping may last through the night, but joy comes with the morning.

LIVE BY FAITH AND NOT BY SIGHT

Faith is a Divine transaction, expressing itself through the love of Jesus. The joy of the Lord is your strength. Resist fear. It cannot hold you back unless you permit it to prevent you from moving forward into God's purpose and plan for your life.

Jesus, today, (and every day) we thank You for what You did on the cross for all humanity. You took our sins and reversed and removed every curse by rescuing Your children, and defeating Satan, once and for all on the cross. We praise and glorify You Jesus, that through Your dying on the cross, and being raised on the third day, You gifted us life, in and through You, forever more.

Rest is trusting God. It is not a lack of activity. Rest is a deep knowing in your heart and soul that God has gone before. Rest in God means not leaning on your own understanding. And not being influenced by your emotions which fluctuate and are fickle.

Your attitude today influences your tomorrows. Trust God in every circumstance. Going deeper in your spiritual journey, means coming up higher, in Christ, which represents His authority to overcome every struggle, not in the flesh, but in, and through His Spirit.

SCRIPTURE:
Proverbs 3: 5-7 TPT
5.Trust in the Lord completely, and do not rely on your own opinions. With all your heart rely on him to guide you, and he will lead you in every decision you make. 6.Become intimate with him in whatever you do, and he will lead you wherever you go. 7.Don't think for a moment that you know it all, for wisdom comes when you adore him with undivided devotion and avoid everything that's wrong.

WEARY, BUT NOT DEFEATED

Just when you thought it was over and your dreams, diminished, that's a lie from the pit of hell. In a season of a lengthy battle, you have become battle weary. The struggle to rise above what you are experiencing appears endless.

You need to silence the voices in your head that are attempting to convince you that your resources are depleted, I can do all this through him who gives me strength, Philippians 4:13 NIV.

God is restoring what you thought was dead. He is breathing His life and hope into you and the purpose He has given you. Don't give up. Don't give in. Be encouraged. Look up.

Square your shoulders, lift your hands to heaven in surrender to God. Go forward unafraid as God is the Alpha and Omega. Be at peace.

You have the Creator of the Universe residing in you as a born-again believer, stop striving, stop stressing. God has got it. Go to sleep tonight and every night in peace as God works behinds the scenes to bring you victory. Stop your ceaseless mental activity. You have the mind of Christ.

SCRIPTURE:
1 Corinthians 2:16 ESV
"For who has understood the mind of the Lord so as to instruct him?" But we have the mind of Christ.

SOOTHING AND SERENE

Allow God's Spirit, His Holy Spirit to breathe new life into you, into your dreams, and into the things you thought were over and lifeless, receive His freshness and refreshing Spirit to fan a flame from the embers of your soul. Take time out to 'be' and not to over 'do'.

Step off from the unrealistic expectations that not only others expect of you, but you endlessly peak your performance on a tiring treadmill of approval and a desire to be accepted by everyone. Stop it.

Seasons predict change. If something isn't working in your life, God is more than likely finished with it. Dismount the dead horse. You're worth more than the time invested in attempting to impress those around you, perhaps with the 'wrong' crowd. Friendships are seasonal too.

I'm not suggesting you simply 'give up' on friends, but spend time quietly in God's presence, evaluating what and who needs to be released from your life, applying Godly wisdom. And move on. Now the Lord is the Spirit, and where the Spirit of the Lord is, there is freedom. 2 Corinthians 3:17 NIV.

SCRIPTURE:
Joel 2:28-29 AMP
28."It shall come about after this that I shall pour out My Spirit on all mankind; and your sons and your daughters will prophesy, your old men will dream dreams, your young men will see visions." 29."Even on the male and female servants I will pour out My Spirit in those days."

AGAINST ALL ODDS

Why remain the same? Explore new territories, move on up and out! Expand your horizons, stop living in restricted thinking. Encounter God, draw into intimacy with Him by putting Him first.

If you remain in a posture of procrastination and fear, consider how much you could accomplish, if you faced your fears head on. Step by step, with cautious momentum, start advancing into your God-given destination.

Be the voice God has given you. His voice to love, to nurture and to serve others into a foundation of hope that will propel them out of their 'stuck' circumstances, into a life of awe and wonder that God has intended for them! You, in Christ, are the solution to someone else's problem!

Lean into somebody's life to listen and not to judge, also, to equip, empower and educate them into an awareness of their identity that is in Christ Jesus. Praise God for His love being poured out for all humanity. Peace on all the earth, in Him, for Him, through Him!

Against all odds, stand your ground! Opposition bows its knee to Jesus Christ.

SCRIPTURE:
Acts 20:24 ESV
But I do not account my life of any value nor as precious to myself, if only I may finish my course and the ministry that I received from the Lord Jesus, to testify to the gospel of the grace of God.

DO IT AFRAID

Invest in your time wisely! It will reap great rewards. No matter what it takes, in Christ, you can do it. Whatever 'it' is, it's no bigger than God. Perhaps you have been sitting on the sideline for some time, waiting for something to happen. Nothing happens by circumstance, or inactivity.

Irrespective of how hard you may be praying for change, God will work with you, in changing you, but there are times when you need to get up and get out and deal with the issues that are attempting to intimidate you, that are keeping you hidden and silent.

In Christ you are a history maker, a world changer and more than a conqueror, you need to be bold, in Christ, stop hiding and hoping for something that is going to happen. Hope and faith involve Godly wisdom and action.

You activate your faith by doing whatever it is you need to do, by doing it afraid, you conquer fear by deliberately moving forward and going out and accomplishing what God is calling you to do! And each time you make up your mind you are going to purposefully pursue God's will for your life, it becomes easier. Fear diminishes over a period of time.

If you are praying for exposure, and you are hiding, you know there will be no result. People don't know you are there, irrespective of how talented you are. It is time for you to make a move! In Christ, you can do it! Make up your mind today to move forward.

SCRIPTURE:
Psalm 23:4 NIV
Even though I walk through the darkest valley, I will fear no evil, for you are with me, your rod and your staff, they comfort me.

LIFTING THE BURDEN

When you realise the weight and the burden of what you are carrying is too much for you, reflect on what Jesus did for you and all humanity. Thank You Jesus for accomplishing everything on the cross! You gave hope to the hopeless and You became a Father to the Fatherless! In Him you are forgiven. In Christ, you have a Higher Calling.

Thank You Jesus. You gave sight to the blind, You have set the captives free, and You have healed the broken hearted! And You have given a voice to the voiceless.

Be encouraged,
The wait may be long,
But in Christ you have been made strong,
With each passing day,
God will reveal the way,
If your burden is heavy,
It is time to surrender the weight of your wait to God.
He will renew your strength and secure your footsteps until you're strong and steady!

Putting things into perspective, God is purging your past from you! It's painful, but it is God's purpose to heal you so you can be used by Him to transform other people's lives!

SCRIPTURE:
Isaiah 41:13 TPT
I am Yahweh, your mighty God! I grip your right hand and won't let you go! I whisper to you: 'Don't be afraid; I am here to help you!'

TURN THE OTHER CHEEK

You could be in a situation that is tricky and involves sensitivity, whether it be professionally or on a personal level. It's so easy to speak from what is on your heart. Where are your heart and your thoughts taking you? For as he thinketh in his heart, so is he: Eat and drink, saith he to thee; but his heart is not with thee, Proverbs 23:7 KJV

In situations where words are flying freely, as God's Word commands, 20.My child, pay attention to what I say. Listen carefully to my words. 21.Don't lose sight of them. Let them penetrate deep into your heart, 22.for they bring life to those who find them, and healing to their whole body. 23.Guard your heart above all else, for it determines the course of your life. 24.Avoid all perverse talk; stay away from corrupt speech. Proverbs 4:20-24 NLT.

Let's choose to love and appreciate each other unconditionally! Too many words spoken in the heat of the moment come at a cost. Is it worth causing division and living from a heart rooted in bitterness, where you seek revenge?

Come clean with God, with yourself and with others. Forgive. You cannot carry that burden of unforgiveness without consequences. Trust God. Praise Him for His healing power.

SCRIPTURE:
Matthew 5:38-40 NIV
38.You have heard that it was said, 'Eye for eye, and tooth for tooth.' 39.But I tell you, do not resist an evil person. If anyone slaps you on the right cheek, turn to them the other cheek also. 40.And if anyone wants to sue you and take your shirt, hand over your coat as well.

BE AWARE OF WHAT YOU ATTRACT

What resides in you will attract that which is in the atmosphere around you. If you are experiencing bitterness, resentment and unforgiveness or any other toxic thoughts, like-minded people will more than likely gather close to you.

It is not only relevant, but essential to redefine your thought life and, by reading and studying God's Word, allowing God to transform your thoughts. If your mind is in chaos, you will attract, or be drawn to chaos that is in close proximity. A holy heart and pure thoughts are as vital as your heartbeat.

What, and who are you allowing to steal your joy? Who has attempted to cut in on your lane? Have you been overlooked, and do you feel rejected and abandoned?

As real as your emotions are, if you permit them to, they will hold you hostage with the drama and trauma involved with whatever has happened to you. I am convinced you do not want to remain glued to your past, and neither your past glued to you.

With God's help, forgive unconditionally and release your thinking from the imprisonment and punishment you have allowed Satan to sting you with.

Words and actions can sting like a wasp, Satan uses those circumstances to pressurise you to withdraw and recoil and conform to a foetal posture, mentally and emotionally.

BE AWARE OF WHAT YOU ATTRACT

You were created to be the difference, in Christ Jesus. Stop permitting Satan from having the upper hand. He has been defeated by Jesus Christ on the cross.

As a born-again believer, walk in Christ-like authority. Behold, I have given you authority to tread on serpents and scorpions, and over all the power of the enemy, and nothing shall hurt you. Luke 10:19 ESV.

There is no going back. Resist being a victim of circumstance, instead, live in your True Identity, in Jesus Christ. Jesus came to set the captives free. Allow hope and expectancy to rise in you today.

When you reach out to those who are desperate around you, you lose sight of your circumstances. God heals you when you make yourself available to someone who is in need. Be intentional about recognising the sometimes, desperate needs of others alongside you. Be kind. Be patient. Be generous with your time and talents. Have compassion.

SCRIPTURE:
Mark: 16-17-18 AMP
17.These signs will accompany those who have believed: in My name they will cast out demons, they will speak in new tongues; 18.they will pick up serpents, and if they drink anything deadly, it will not hurt them; they will lay hands on the sick, and they will get well.

THE WIND BENEATH YOUR WINGS

In seasons of exhaustion, when you have given your all you have to give, it is time to take a break. You have been working long hours, perhaps you feel you need to because of your financial situation. You go to bed with anxious thoughts circulating around in your head. The Devil whispers to your soul, well, what are you going to do? You know what to do.

Settle your soul in a quiet space and place, rest in God's presence and wait with expectancy for His quiet whisper. Life is hectic enough without you adding to the accelerated pace of living. You need to take stock of where you are at, one moment at a time.

When you are in a whirlwind with so much occupying your mind, thoughts of desperation attempt to bombard your thinking patterns. Satan's intention is to wear you out. In Christ, take authority over Satan's lure to distract you.

It is imperative you calmly look at your situation and recognise what your urgent need is. If it involves finances and expenses, my suggestion is to be increasingly intentional regarding how you can budget more effectively. Where can you cut your expenses that will free you up financially, which will take some weight off your mind?

If you don't scrutinise your circumstances from God's perspective, you will magnify the situation and invite fear. You need to be solution focused and consider alternative methods in becoming more financially secure.

THE WIND BENEATH YOUR WINGS

Unwanted expenses manifest themselves at the most inconvenient time, but God is the supplier of all your needs. And my God will supply every need of yours according to his riches in glory in Christ Jesus, Philippians 4:19 ESV.

Allow the Wind of the Spirit to elevate you. Slipstreaming in the stratosphere far over and above your circumstances. Be high and lifted in Christ.

When you trust God and take your anxiety into the Light and Truth of Jesus Christ, the situations that once had power over you, the lies of Satan, which attempted to trap your mind and heart in a tight grip are now loosed by the authority of heaven. Every curse is reversed in the Name of Jesus.

Coming out of any situation, on the road to recovery, requires seeing the Light and Truth of Jesus in every dark circumstance. Praise God for His victory and ask Him to heal you of whatever has been a stronghold in your life. Where the Spirit of the Lord is, there is freedom.

Go forward, in Christ, bright, bold, beautiful, and quietly confident in Him who has already accomplished everything for you, living in the outcome of the cross and from His resurrection power that dwells within you, as a born-again believer.

SCRIPTURE:
Psalm 150:6 NIV
Let everything that has breath praise the Lord. Praise the Lord.

YOU ARE PROTECTED

Irrespective of how you may be feeling at this present moment, I urge you not to succumb to your feelings and emotions as they are fickle, they fluctuate, and they're unpredictable from one minute to the next.

Feelings and emotions exhaust you, because you are wanting to listen to what your flesh is demanding of you, and you cannot fulfil the needs of those demands. So, you feel less than, insecure, and unable to do what you think is expected of you, perhaps even unrealistic expectations are put on you.

At the same time, you are bottled up with emotions and you know you cannot trust yourself to express your feelings effectively, as your emotions have been compressed for so long that it would be like releasing a champagne cork, if you started opening your mouth to speak.

You have thoughts for words (that attempt to squeeze the life from you) and deep down, in some cases, you feel you have the right for revenge, but vengeance belongs to God. Beloved, never avenge yourselves, but leave the way open for God's wrath [and His judicial righteousness]; for it is written [in Scripture], "Vengeance is Mine, I will repay," says the Lord. Romans 12:19, AMP.

Also, you cannot fool your body for too long as your feelings and emotions have roots, as the Bible calls them roots of bitterness, which lead to resentment and unforgiveness, and could result in consequences regarding your health.

YOU ARE PROTECTED

People have mistreated you, you've been overlooked, misunderstood, you have chosen to gain strides of revenge by not co-operating with those around you, or you remain silent. You attempt to punish those close to you, by keeping them guessing regarding your silence and indifference.

Toxic thoughts harden your heart, making it impenetrable. A calloused heart is like the hardening of arteries where the blood cannot be transported around the body effectively. Hatred, unspoken words of poison and the like, are reversible and curable when you surrender your heart and life to Jesus.

Only He can be your Spiritual Surgeon, and cut, piece by piece, tenderly using His scalpel, and removing every fibre of pain and poison in your soul and heart. It is imperative for you to take ownership of your current state of thinking.

As I am on the road to recovery, I'm speaking the truth in love, as God's Word says, Instead, speaking the truth in love, we will grow to become in every respect the mature body of him who is the head, that is, Christ. Ephesians 4:15 NIV. Stop attempting to mask your pain, do not short-change yourself.

Your behaviour reflects your inner life, in the way you feel guilty and your urge to be noticed. I know the signs of deep insecurity and the need to be loved by people who cannot love you or acknowledge you, only God can do that. I encourage you to refrain from looking at humans for all your needs to be met, because only God can fulfil what your heart is longing for.

YOU ARE PROTECTED

Only God can heal your hurt and pain, His love is the antidote for the years that your life has been deeply rooted in pain that has caused you to feel unloved.

As previously written, I am well acquainted with that behaviour, that is why I am wanting you to come clean regarding being honest with yourself and God, by starting a new life in Christ.

Therefore, if anyone is in Christ, the new creation has come: The old has gone, the new is here! 2 Corinthians 5:17 NIV. You are worth more than where you are at this moment. You are not in a bad place, but God has more for you, pray bold prayers, and draw into intimacy, in Christ. Seek God's face, soak in His presence. Be still and know that I am God, Psalm 46:10, NIV.

Every little thing is going to be okay. The trials and tribulations, when you persist in growing in Christ, will strengthen your walk and faith in God, which will lead you to become triumphant and victorious, in Christ.

SCRIPTURE:
Psalm 91:4 TPT
His massive arms are wrapped around you, protecting you. You can run under his covering of majesty and hide. His arms of faithfulness are a shield keeping you from harm.

SOW SEEDS OF KINDNESS

In every situation, sow seeds of kindness. A heart cultivated in love, watered gently by generosity and compassion, and nurtured appropriately, produces prolific blossoms and blooms as it reaps a harvest influenced by love, joy, peace, patience, kindness, goodness, faithfulness, gentleness, and self-control, the Fruit of the Spirit.

Cultivate your heart in the love of God. Pay particular attention to your thoughts, prevent them from leading you from the narrow path that God has assigned for you to walk on. Thoughts become words, which transition into attitudes.

Be careful who you associate with. A handful of role models, including a confidant, people you can trust implicitly, who will, with God's help, provide advice and guide you in your life journey. They are essential in keeping you accountable. Confidantes and role models are also transparent, humble and possess a wealth of experience which cannot be purchased.

Great role models and confidantes are few and far between. They will be honest with you, where and when applicable, because they have lived a considerable time and God has helped them through sticky situations, which you may be experiencing.

They are not there to inflate your pride or ego, but they are used by God to oversee your journey in life. You recognise early, people who leak information, regarding how quickly you'll hear the latest gossip. Stay away from gossip mongers.

SOW SEEDS OF KINDNESS

In sowing seeds of kindness and being led by God, along with suitable role models and confidantes in your life, in Christ, you will become stronger in your decision making. It does not mean you become co-dependent; however confidantes and role models are invaluable. God created humanity for community. In whatever you plant, God does the growing.

Of course, role models and confidantes don't replace God, however, they are equipped to listen to you and groom you for greater things, with God's help. Bearing in mind, sowing seeds of kindness represents servanthood. Who can you equip and empower today, who is in need? You can sow a seed for a need. Become available, and as Jesus did, wash someone's feet today who are weary at this time.

Speak words of refreshment to them. Just being there, doesn't always represent talking, but instead, it could be a time of fine tuning your God-given gift of listening. People are longing to be listened to, and not to be compared and competed with.

SCRIPTURE:
1 Corinthians 3:6-9 NLT
6.I planted the seed in your hearts, and Apollos watered it, but it was God who made it grow. 7.It's not important who does the planting, or who does the watering. What's important is that God makes the seed grow. 8.The one who plants and the one who waters work together with the same purpose. And both will be rewarded for their own hard work. 9.For we are both God's workers. And you are God's field. You are God's building.

REVIVE YOUR SOUL

Today is a gift. It's wonderfully wrapped and perfectly packaged, there's nothing like the present. It is bright and beautiful, just as you are.

May it inspire you as its beauty is unravelled, revealing an inner peace, permeated and powerful. Immensely impacting. Take the time to inhale its heavenly scent, marvel and be intentionally inspired by every miraculous moment today.

Look, listen and learn. Rest, recover and discover, new possibilities, new avenues to explore. Live, laugh and love. Be a dispenser of joy, sprinkle it over every thought, word, and deed, release it, until it overflows from you spontaneously.

Live on purpose for a purpose, live like there is no tomorrow. Today is a creative masterpiece, capture it through God's lens. Freeze frame.

You are encouraged to empower others. Be good to yourself. To revive your soul, it is time to let go of the past, cultivate forgiveness until it becomes a way of life for you. Strengthen your creativity skills.

Resist co-dependency. Be who God created you to be, where you are comfortable in your own skin. Make up your mind to enjoy everyday life.

Extend yourself in becoming an authentic friend. Resist blame-gaming, it complicates matters. The past is the past, move on. Accomplishment involves a cultivation of faith and occupying your God-given territory and destiny.

REVIVE YOUR SOUL

Choose to think good thoughts, thoughts that revive your soul. Intend for them to be spoken as words that escalate enthusiasm for your life, and to overflow into other people around you.

A soul that is worn out and weary yearns for the soft breath of God to breathe freshness and vitality into it, and to restore energy that has leaked from its very existence. And God's Spirit releases hope, clarity, and distinct direction. God is waiting for you to come to Him, to be healed and refreshed.

SCRIPTURE:
Luke 6:38 AMP
Give, and it will be given to you. They will pour into your lap a good measure-pressed down, shaken together, and running over [with no space left for more]. For with the standard of measurement you use [when you do good to others], it will be measured to you in return.

RELEASE INTO PEACE

Fear has paralysed your desire in wanting to gain traction in moving forward to where God intends you to be. I remember taking an opportunity of occupying the aperture of a hot air balloon, capturing something unique.

It was a thrilling moment. Whilst I was standing there, someone attempted to nudge me out of the way. There was only room for one person. I would not surrender to the tactics of intimidation.

If procrastination had taken hold of me, I would not have been able to capture something as extraordinary and extravagant in colour as that hot air balloon.

Preparation and positioning yourself to go beyond where you are at this moment, is paramount in seizing opportunities to walk through open doors. Too often you wait for the doors of opportunity to come to you. Or you are waiting for God to answer your prayers. He is waiting on you to take the first step of faith. You need to walk into your God-given destiny. Be the solution to the circumstances you are in.

God cares for the sparrow, and He knows the hairs on your head. He has contained your tears in a bottle. Your life is in His hands. Surrender all to God that is attempting to hold you back, and make up your mind to move forward, fulfilling your God-given purpose. And, as you do, you will experience God's peace. Within and without. Be at peace, in Christ.

SCRIPTURE:
James 3:18 ESV
And a harvest of righteousness is sown in peace by those who make peace.

MAY THE ROAD RISE TO MEET YOU

May the gentle breath of God breathe His life into your dreams, enlarging your vision and capacity. God's creative brilliance is within you, you're groomed for greatness. Be inspired, invigorated, and amazed, every day, and in everything, give thanks. Celebrate today. Live to forgive.

May the road rise to meet you. May the wind be always at your back. May the sun shine warm upon your face; the rains fall soft upon your fields and until we meet again, may God hold you in the palm of His hand. A traditional Irish blessing.

Discover the goodness of God in every circumstance. Be intentional, every appropriate door is open, waiting to be walked through. Walk through them. Some opportunities involve calculated risks, whilst other doors, you will be led by God's wisdom.

Today is history for God. It gives you peace of mind. Trust God for a good outcome. With God all things are possible. He is a mountain mover; He will give you strategies for victory in each of your battles. No two battles are the same. Seek God's wisdom in how to win each battle effortlessly.

The battle belongs to the Lord. Trust Him. The doors that God has closed and sealed are for a reason, resist the temptation in attempting to open them.

SCRIPTURE
Revelation 3:8 NIV
I know your deeds. See, I have placed before you an open door that no one can shut. I know that you have little strength, yet you have kept my word and have not denied my name.

SOAR LIKE AN EAGLE

Unleash your soul today, release yourself to the beauty of this day. Be inspired and become invigorated by it. Soar like an eagle, walk free, unencumbered. Be good to yourself, forgive others, forgive yourself. Forget what lies behind, release yourself into the beauty of this day.

History is being made today, be part of it. Whatever season you're in, God is with you. Know your season, what is God saying to you regarding the season you are in? He is working things together for your good, and for the good of others in your life. Be immersed in His peace.

Too often you are looking for the next 'big' thing whilst you miss the significance of the smaller happenings in your daily life. Being content is not camping where you are, instead, it's possessing a peaceful mindset, in preparation for what and where God is releasing you into.

Perspective: don't major in the minors. Leave your past behind you. Press toward the mark of perfection God has prepared for you, to bless others. Praise God and be raised.

SCRIPTURE:
Isaiah 30:18 AMP
Therefore the Lord waits [expectantly] and longs to be gracious to you, and therefore He waits on high to have compassion on you. For the Lord is a God of justice; blessed (happy, fortunate) are all those who long for Him [since He will never fail them].

THERE IS LIFE IN THE DESERT

If today was your last day on this earth, what would you do, who would you contact? Life is precious and you are fragile. Live, love and forgive. Do not permit opportunities to bless others to slip through your fingers.

Keep life simple, slipstream through this beautiful day. A desert holds its own fascination. It hosts life beyond description. The landscape is scorched earth, with merciless heat.

There is more to life in a desert which is considered a hostile environment but possessing an instinctiveness to survive. God's provision in situations that are intensely barren and sometimes desperate, are an oasis to the soul.

If you are experiencing what appears to be a desert situation, quench your soul with God's Word. He will lead and guide you into a safe place of shelter, representing an oasis.

God has established a firm foundation in you through humility. You are in the process of being released to fly like an eagle, soaring the thermals. What is your intentionality in your desert seasons? Speak life into your circumstances, by decreeing and declaring God's Word.

SCRIPTURE:
Isaiah 51:3 TPT
Indeed, Yahweh will comfort Zion, restore her, and comfort all her broken places. He will transform her wilderness into the garden of Bliss, her desert into the garden of Yahweh. Joy and laughter will fill the air with thanksgiving and joyous melodies.

SETBACKS ARE COME BACKS

Start the day right, cultivate good thoughts and put them into action by being kind. Do not be deceived. You cannot surrender to your past, in an attempt to accelerate your present/future.

Persevere, when the pressure appears insurmountable, God, by His grace, will equip you to finish your race, and in your lane. Press on. Press through to victory. Never give up. Never give in.

Do not surrender to setbacks, rather use them as comebacks. They are temporary if you decide not to get stuck in circumstances which do not define you. Hope is the vital ingredient which takes authority over the darkness, commanding it to evacuate, enabling the Truth and Light of Jesus Christ to take up residency in your soul.

Live in the wonder of today, capture its miraculous moments as God breathes His life into you. Be amazed, see things through His lens, be original, as you were created to be.

There is no time like the present to be generous to someone you know, releasing encouragement and God's unconditional love into their lives. Food for their soul, and for yours too.

SCRIPTURE:
Romans 8:31-32 AMP
31.What then shall we say to all these things? If God is for us, who can be [successful] against us? 32.He who did not spare [even] His own Son, but gave Him up for us all, how will He not also, along with Him, graciously give us all things?

NEVER GIVE UP

Irrespective of what your circumstances look like, keep on hoping, persist in speaking God's Word and decree and declare hope over your life, and God's Truth will prevail.

Believe in what God has already accomplished in your situation. Stop sitting on tender hooks, expecting the worst-case scenario. That is the scheme of Satan to prevent you from going forward. Opposition bows its knee to Jesus' anointing for breakthrough.

Anxiety is rooted in uncertainty. Be certain of your True Identity in Jesus Christ. Knowing who you are in Christ, diminishes the lure of Satan attempting to keep you trapped.

Be encouraged, your breakthrough is closer than you could imagine, living a God-inspired journey called life. In Christ, you are significant, you are the difference, you add value. Resist distractions that attract insecurity and competitiveness.

You are far greater than that, in Christ Jesus. Stop reducing yourself in the way God created you, by listening to, and believing the lies that are being whispered to you. Reject them, repel them, at their onset, and move on.

Be still your beating heart. For those who are experiencing a midnight hour, God's hand is over you. He will never leave you, nor forsake you. Be encouraged. Be expectant. Be elevated in your thinking.

Mind mechanisms: There is no going back once a decision has been made. Never miss a God-given opportunity to bless someone and to move forward into your breakthrough, with relentless hope.

NEVER GIVE UP

Exhaustive emotions are a result of attempting to solve complicated issues in your own strength. Seeing situations through tired eyes of the soul usually magnifies the circumstance you are in. It's imperative to take stock and to establish where you can simplify your life in order to reduce stress, with God's help.

Also, I encourage you to write a list of victories in your life, scenarios that looked impossible in the natural, yet God came through for you. It may not have been in the way you had hoped, but God knows what is best for you.

Calm the thoughts in your mind by immediately recognising trouble shooting issues that can be resolved by God's grace. You will no longer be a servant to fear, dread, disappointment or any other emotions that have keep you captive for far too long. This is your breakthrough moment. Laugh. Love. Forgive.

SCRIPTURE:
Psalm 37:34 NLT
Put your hope in the Lord. Travel steadily along his path. He will honor you by giving you the land. You will see the wicked destroyed.

PEACEFUL AUTHORITY

Jesus, the Prince of Peace residing in your soul, takes authority over the chaos attempting to spin out of control in your circumstances. Peace within, represents clarity. You have authority in Christ to move mountains and to inform the mountains of how big God is.

You have literally been trembling with fear over things that have attempted to hold you captive. This must stop. When you open your mouth and speak God's Word in absolute belief and trust in Him, by saying to the devil, 'It is written', as Jesus spoke to Satan, the atmosphere will change from chaos to peace.

Command and declare the storms in your life to evacuate and in their place, to be replaced with the occupancy, residence, inhabitation and possession of the Prince of Peace, Jesus Christ, to rule richly in your heart. Go into this miraculous day, in His peace, ushering in His Presence.

Paint your world with peace, love, and joy. Today is woven with miraculous moments, capture them. Sing, dance, love and laugh like you have never done before. Seize the day and every opportunity to grow in Christ, and to bless others.

SCRIPTURE:
Mark 11:22-24 TPT
22.Jesus replied, "Let the faith of God be in you! 23.Listen to the truth I speak to you: Whoever says to this mountain with great faith and does not doubt, 'Mountain, be lifted up and thrown into the midst of the sea,' and believes that what he says will happen, it will be done. 24.This is the reason I urge you to boldly believe for whatever you ask for in prayer-be convinced that you have received it and it will be yours."

NOBODY WINS AN ARGUMENT

I encourage you to release God's love and mercy when people have a different viewpoint from you. Judgment and criticism can wound the soul, and careless words are not worth it. Hurting people hurt people.

Pride and self-righteousness come at a cost in distancing yourself from people. For some, you like to argue and attract those who do the same.

Perhaps you developed an argumentative spirit growing up in a household where you needed to defend yourself. And, also, you probably weren't listened to. Deep within your soul you resolved that you were not going to ignored, at any cost.

In the scheme of things, what does it matter if someone disagrees with your point of view? In the light of eternity, it's not worth the burden and weight of offense and resentment.

Life is too precious and fragile to waste it on petty differences of opinion. Unity is strength, let it go, including all toxic thoughts, permit Christ's peace to flow, within your soul and the atmosphere you are in.

You need to grow from your challenges and to attract and bless individuals who stimulate you with their differences, and to stir each other up with encouragement, leaning in and listening to what the other person's perspective is.

If someone sees the same thing differently from you, they are not rejecting you. To be honest, they are entitled to their own opinion. Control and manipulation bind you, be discerning regarding that behaviour and mindset.

NOBODY WINS AN ARGUMENT

Ask God to heal you and to set you free from such emotions. Besides, you are bigger than, and better off, without always having the last word. Choose to adjust your mind posture regarding how other people perceive life, even if it isn't easy for you to understand their point of view.

Don't walk away from something that is about to bring change, for good. Be intentional about shining brightly for someone today, a contrast from nit picking and producing strife. You will start to flourish in a calm environment, there is no looking back. You are worth more than that.

Miscarried dreams do not represent failure, instead, they are a pivotal point in being directed to, and walking in, God's divine alignment. It is time to occupy and possess your God-given destiny and to stop 'camping' on your excuses. Freedom: Doing new things expecting exceptional results. Be the salt and light in Christ, today and always.

SCRIPTURE:
Psalm 34:14 NIV
Turn from evil and do good; seek peace and pursue it.

KEEP YOUR HEAD ABOVE THE WATER

This message is for someone who is almost 'drowning' in the shallows. God keeps putting this on my heart for you.

You think it's over. You're convinced your dreams have died. You consider your present/future to represent a miscarriage of hope, do not believe that lie from Satan. You are weary from the fight of keeping your head above the water, even though the message here is, you can drown in the shallows.

By that I mean, if you look at your current circumstances, in the natural, they appear to be hopeless. Seeing things in the everyday, can attract a host of emotions and feelings that are unwanted, but when you add God's Super to your natural, everything changes.

Do not be discouraged, irrespective of how dire your situation is at this moment. Look up and seek God's help. He is waiting for you to move, and to act in faith.

Dust yourself off. Pick yourself up. Build yourself up in the Lord. You're closer to your miracle than you think. Be blessed. Be at peace. Stay strong in the Lord. Keep walking and rejoicing in Him.

Look at how far God has brought you, why would you want to surrender to what appears to be chaotic, confusing, and irreparable? Quieten your soul by shifting your thoughts to peace and calm, in Christ.

God has got your situation in His hands, but each time you fret and experience anxiety, you are taking control of that incident, which means God cannot do anything whilst you are sweating it out. God never sleeps. Anxiety and worry deprive you of your sleep.

KEEP YOUR HEAD ABOVE THE WATER

You need to develop a good sleeping pattern, to eat healthy food and to exercise your body and your mind, focusing on the good things in life that are of God.

Be rest assured, you are not a product of your past, your past does not influence or determine your future, and you are not who people think, or say you are.

In Christ, you are more than that. Rejection is re-direction, bless those who have rejected you, move on and occupy your God-given territory. Change does not come without opposition. But, in Christ, you have the victory. There is victory in the camp, claim it. Walk in it.

SCRIPTURE:
Deuteronomy 20:4 ESV
'For the Lord your God is he who goes with you to fight for you against your enemies, to give you the victory.'

STOP BEING A SLAVE TO YOUR PAST

God is bigger than what you're experiencing. Be encouraged. Be at peace. Be good to yourself. Be kind to others. The joy of the Lord is your strength.

Momentum: Resist reducing God to your limited thinking. Dreams are conceived, cultivated, and transitioned into reality when your faith in Jesus is activated. You become a slave to the things that master you. Stop it.

Be refreshed and rejuvenated, the tide is coming in. Stop striving. What does that mean to you? Tide and time wait for no one. Don't procrastinate, be directional, refuse fear which could be attempting to hold you back.

In everything and with everyone, bless and do not curse, resist the flesh, instead, cultivate the Fruit of the Spirit. Harness your emotions and your thoughts, bring them in line with God's will for your life.

Drink every drop of goodness in this day. Make lemonade from lemons, which is a vital attitude adjustment. Live and love on purpose. Carpe Diem.

SCRIPTURE:
Romans 6:16 AMP
Do you not know that when you *continually* offer yourselves to someone to do his will, you are the slaves of the one whom you obey, either [slaves] of sin, which leads to death, or of obedience, which leads to righteousness (right standing with God)?

IN CHRIST YOU ARE INDESCRUCTIBLE

Ride the wave of faith. Resist distractions from dismantling your peace and exhausting you. Don't permit anyone or any circumstance to short-change you of your peace, in Christ.

God's peace is your umpire which will equip and empower you to navigate through troubled waters. Perfect peace cannot be purchased. Peace is God's gift to humanity through Jesus Christ, Who is God in the flesh, yet, without sinning.

A selfless sacrifice He made on the cross, to restore humankind. Rest in His peace, permit His peace to revive your soul. Immerse yourself in God's Word, soaking your soul and spirit in His Light and Truth. God's Truth will reveal your direction and strengthen your identity in Christ.

Co-dependency weakens your God-given ability to co-operate with His Holy Spirit in every situation, where God will not only supply all your needs, but He will equip you in coming out victorious in situations that looked bleak and impossible. And Jesus said to him, "'If you can'! All things are possible for one who believes." Mark 9:23 ESV.

Your present journey appears lonely and the gradient, steep, but the more resistance that comes against you, particularly regarding change, God, by His grace, will see you through and set your feet on higher ground. Yes, feast on all the treasures of the heavenly realm and fill your thoughts with heavenly realities, and not with the distractions of the natural realm. Colossians 3:2 TPT.

IN CHRIST YOU ARE INDESCRUCTIBLE

You will recognise the tactics of Satan, attempting to prevent you from going forward and moving into your God-given purpose and destiny. There is no going back. Be rest assured you were created for a time such as this.

Move on, move up and move out of your stale thinking into new territory and to new heights, in Christ. You are stronger than you think you are. With God's help, you have overcome incredible hurdles that you never thought possible. When you are in the eye of a storm, keep your eyes on God.

2.{Looking away from all that will distract us and] focusing our eyes on Jesus, who is the Author and Perfector of faith [the first incentive for our belief and the One who brings our faith to maturity], who for the joy [of accomplishing the goal] set before Him endured the cross, disregarding the shame, and sat down at the right hand of the throne of God [revealing His deity, His authority, and the completion of His work]. Hebrews 12:2 AMP.

God is with you even though you think He isn't near, do not surrender to your emotions. Be fixed and focused on God's assignment for your life. Your greatest moments are in the going through as God is strengthening you and healing your heart and your soul of brokenness.

SCRIPTURE
Mark 3:15 NIV
And to have authority to drive out demons.

CHANGE STARTS WITH A NEW CHAPTER

Stop grieving over, or longing for the things that God is finished with. It is important to recognise the season you are in and to learn as much as you can from it.

You know when you are coming to the end of your season, as God takes the desire to do the things that have been easy and enjoyable for you, they don't hold the same attraction as they used to.

It is not always the flesh that influences your choices and decisions. Attempting to prolong your current season could be because you are comfortable. With time, your level of comfort becomes discomfort in that same situation which suggests staleness has set in.

Recognise when things are not be as fresh as they used to be. And make your move in a new direction. Opportunities emerge through opposition.

Choose to sail away in today, peaceful, and powerful. Take authority over your mountains. The breath of God's creative brilliance is like a soft whisper seeping through your soul and spirit, catch it.

Look at life differently. Not every day is the same, routine is recycled thinking. Be creative, capture this day through an excellent lens of clarity, and direction. You reap what you sow.

Emerge, expect, and experience excellence. Change is a heartbeat away, choose to be the change. Be encouraged. You are the difference in this day, live it.

CHANGE STARTS WITH A NEW CHAPTER

Rest your mind and your mouth, when necessary, be still and recharge. Sow a seed for a need. Water it with God's Word. Watch it grow. Head up. Shoulders back. Your arms raised in total surrender to God.

Whatever challenges you may experience when you have decided to let go of the things that have held you back, they will not distract you as you have made up your mind to gain momentum and to occupy new territory.

New beginnings will not pose a threat, instead you will view and negotiate each step of the way with a positive attitude and a hopeful heart. Keep on moving in Christ, you were created for a time such as this. Do not pay attention to the naysayers and be wise as to whom you confide in with regards to your new adventures and exciting life opportunities.

SCRIPTURE:
2 Peter 3:13 NLT
But we are looking forward to the new heavens and new earth he has promised, a world filled with God's righteousness.

CAREFREE, IN CHRIST

Your True Identity is in Jesus Christ, and It's not who you think you are, but knowing Whose you are. For those who have been experiencing intense opposition, you are exhausted and seeking clarity, God is preparing you for breakthrough.

Every beautiful, significant thing in this day,
Is an invitation to settle, relax, to be at peace –
Let it have it's say,
Every moment is momentous and miraculous,
In a heartbeat, absorb the warmth of kindness.
In haste there is too much to miss,
Draw from the wealth of this day not in a financial way,
But what you are being taught,
All intensity evacuated and solace sought!
In exchange, release kindness to those around you,
It's not just what you say, but what you do
That makes a significant difference between ordinary and extraordinary,
Weaving a beautiful story.

SCRIPTURE:
Deuteronomy 12:28 AMP
"Be careful to listen to all these words which I am commanding you, so that it may be well with you and with your children after you forever, because you will be doing what is good and right in the sight of the Lord your God."

JOY DOETH GOOD LIKE A MEDICINE

Live, laugh and love, often. Nehemiah said, "Go and enjoy choice food and sweet drinks, and send some to those who have nothing prepared. This day is holy to our Lord. Do not grieve, for the joy of the Lord is your strength." Nehemiah 8:10, NIV. Joy represents authority, in Christ, walk in it daily.

When circumstances are swirling around you, and you are joy-filled, you resist giving power to the devil. Your life, lived in the authority of Christ, represents contentment, peace, and purpose.

Move into the purpose God has assigned for you. No holding back. Let go of your yesteryears. They are not the good old days as the saying goes, that is a representation of living in nostalgia which drags you back into your past and siphons God's joy from your soul and spirit. You are over that.

Resist distractions. Attract every good thing by focusing sharply on what God is intending for you to accomplish. Run with what is in your hands, don't keep it all for yourself.

Count your blessings and take authority over 'self'. Thoughts: Mechanisms of the mind, train your brain to draw power from the positive and to be at peace with yourself.

When you are at peace with you, you're at peace with the world. People will respond or react to the way you identify yourself.

Branch out into the brilliance of today. Say or do something special that will be remembered for future generations. Sharpen your focus through God's lens. The distractions will simply 'fall' away.

JOY DOETH GOOD LIKE A MEDICINE

For the kingdom of God is not a matter of eating and drinking [what one likes], but of righteousness and peace and joy in the Holy Spirit, Romans 14:17 AMP. Living in the righteousness of God, peace, and joy will become a way of life for you.

To be honest, until you decide to 'cultivate' the Spirit of God's joy, you give power to Satan to intimidate and control you. However, when you walk and talk in agreement with the Spirit of joy, (all God's Fruit of the Spirit, Galatians 5:22-23), and God's Word, you choose to live in the rhythm of God's heartbeat where nothing can confiscate your joy and peace, in Christ.

Circumstances that used to frustrate you, you'll recognise early, however, you now choose to laugh at the ploys of the devil. I am not making light-hearted of serious situations. But, even, in your midnight hour, choose to praise God.

SCRIPTURE:
Proverbs 15:13 MSG
A cheerful heart brings a smile to your face; a sad heart makes it hard to get through the day.

FORGIVENESS IS FREEING

Your heart is aching resulting from loss, a loss of a relationship that went sour. The person walked away without any explanation. You have tried everything in your power to make amends, but nothing changes.

You have probably been beating yourself up mentally and verbally, blaming yourself for something that perhaps God meant for your good.

The situation you're in, could be more complicated and painful than words can express, particularly if it involves a family member. But you cannot drown in your source of pain.

It is easy for me to write and remark on walking away and forgetting the agonising moments. The longing you have for that person or people to return to what was so special and familiar, is almost unbearable. It isn't easy, and neither is it always possible.

But what was, cannot replace what God has purposed for you. It does not make sense what happened. But, so often, hurting people hurt people. Don't scrutinise every conservation to draw on conclusions that could lead you on a rabbit trail.

My suggestion is to take your pain to God first and foremost, He is waiting for you to surrender your experience and to heal you. Healing of the heart takes time, and it is painful at times, but It is worth it.

FORGIVENESS IS FREEING

It is a human tendency to draw comfort from people, I am not suggesting you're not to do that, but more often than not, human reactions are complicated and can aggravate the situation, and the pain you are experiencing.

People mean well, but it may not be the right time to discuss your raw emotions until you are stronger, both mentally and emotionally. It's best to leave it with God.

You cannot bury your feelings or emotions; it is unhealthy to do so. But, at the same time, you can overtalk the situation until it wears other people out as well. In tricky relationships, it is best to give freedom to the other person, by stopping your urge to rekindle the heated conversation. Let it go.

You don't know what they are going through, and what they are processing does not make sense to you, I understand that, but more importantly, God does too. Toxic thoughts permeate your soul if you permit them to. Admittedly, the pain is real, but you need to keep the main thing the main thing.

Pain can dominate your thinking; it is important you deal with the pain as I mentioned, by communicating with God. I recommend you go for walks, journal, read and study God's Word and read good Christian books, listen to music, form new friendships. Do not become stuck in the moment.

FORGIVENESS IS FREEING

Time is a healer. You need to permit yourself to heal as God touches your soul and transforms your thinking. Immerse your soul in God's Word. Release that person, in love, speaking poison from a wounded, limping soul, is what you drink, which is intended for the other person or people.

Words rooted in pain will influence your decision to drink that poison, whilst they are enjoying life, totally unaware of your bitterness, resentment, and offence. Stop permitting your poisonous thoughts to consume you. It is not worth it.

Forgiveness sets you free. Lift your voice against those 'voices' in your mind that are resisting change. Splash your world with God's love, joy, and His peace.

Now the Lord is the Spirit, and where the Spirit of the Lord is, there is freedom, 2 Corinthians 3:17 ESV.

SCRIPTURE:
Hebrews 4:15 ESV
For we do not have a high priest who is unable to sympathize with our weaknesses, but one who in every respect has been tempted as we are, yet without sin.

CHANGES ARE CHALLENGING BUT WORTH IT

You are hoping for change, but change is manifested when you make a choice to walk away from people who have not been a healthy influence in your life. This is not blaming anyone; however, It is easy to become accustomed to, and being comfortable with the 'same old' way of doing life, with the same people.

Or, alternatively, you need to walk away from situations that could potentially attract some sort of unwanted influence in your decision making.

Change, in whatever form, involves adaptability, a freeing up of your mind, a willingness to embrace new possibilities. Stale thinking, resonating with your past, could be holding you back. I am not recommending you make an impulsive move which could result in a more complicated scenario, without good results.

Deep down inside, God created you for change. As you mature, embracing new mindsets are almost overwhelming, taking technology, as an example. But if you don't move with the times, you will get left behind. This is not an attempt to coerce you into making decisions you are uncomfortable with.

A suggestion would be to frame your mind with new possibilities of moving forward, whatever that represents to you. Picture yourself in a new environment, with new friends. If you are an introvert, I realise that is not easy for you.

CHANGES ARE CHALLENGING BUT WORTH IT

You can talk yourself out of exceptional possibilities regarding gaining ground, in moving forward. Instead, pursue and discover new possibilities that can become a reality for you.

Do not permit fear to hold you back. Can you imagine where you could go and the new heights you can achieve by believing in what God has purposed for you, to bless you, and others around you?

Discover what God has already prepared for you as you break free from the limitations associated with former mindsets. Step out from the shadows and occupy your Divine inheritance. Life goes by too quickly, don't procrastinate. Whatever you invest in today will influence your tomorrow.

Stop recycling stale thinking and mindsets, in an attempt to make them new. God is finished with the old. Step out into the deep. Freshen your God-given vision with new eyes.

SCRIPTURE:
John 21:6 NIV
He said, "Throw your net on the right side of the boat and you will find some." When they did, they were unable to haul the net in because of the large number of fish.

LIFE IS PRECIOUS

To the young, I say don't procrastinate. And to the mature, it's not too late. I encourage you today if you're 'stuck' where you are at, build yourself up in the Lord, by speaking life into your situation, advance and occupy new territory, and cross the finish line. In Christ, you can do all things.

You may have had words of negativity spoken over your life as a child, and as an adult, even as a mature adult, you are still being squeezed by those words, after all this time. Forgive whoever spoke those words to you, let them go, in the love of Christ. Stop permitting your mind to be arrested by your past.

As you free the other person, you unshackle yourself from the principalities and dominions of hell. You free yourself, in Christ. Move on, upwards, onwards, and outwards. The sky is your limit. You were created for a time such as this.

Ephesians 4:26-27 TPT. 26.But don't let the passion of your emotions lead you to sin! Don't let anger control you or be fuel for revenge, not for even a day. 27.Don't give the slanderous accuser, the Devil, an opportunity to manipulate you!

There is no time like the present, it's a gift. To those who are hesitant and have held back, break free from limitations. Your history does not define you, or your present/future. Life is precious, forgive, laugh, and love.

LIFE IS PRECIOUS

Don't waste your time and energy on the 'what ifs' and the 'should have been' moments, those emotions that are steeped in regret and remorse. Stop giving people power over your life as their conversations are dominated by guilt and condemnation. Speak less, love more, forgive quickly, move to higher ground, in Christ.

Forgiveness will thaw your heart when it is cultivated in the love of God. A tender touch, a sincere smile, a kind word changes the atmosphere, a shed tear, joy released-evacuating fear, whilst you draw others near. Look for the exceptional in everything and in everyone.

Stepping out. What could be holding you back from God's plan and purpose for your life?

SCRIPTURE:
Ephesians 6:12 TPT
Your hand-to-hand combat is not with human beings, but with the highest principalities and authorities operating in rebellion under the heavenly realms. For they are a powerful class of demon-gods and evil spirits that hold this dark world in bondage.

GOD IS WITH YOU

Recently, on a photo shoot, whilst I was standing waist deep in the Arrow River, Arrowtown, New Zealand, the force of the river resisted my being there. Carefully I navigated through the intense areas of power that attempted to reduce me to fear. But I would not surrender.

With God's help, I discovered a tranquil spot in that fast-flowing river, which enabled me to capture the magnificence of His creation. The scene represented God's peace in a storm. Christ in you, will equip you in overcoming the mountains in your life, which you thought were insurmountable.

Do not surrender to fear nor become distracted by the devil. It's his intention and leverage to exhaust you. Exhaustive emotions are not your identity in Christ. How do you perceive yourself? Does your past persistently regurgitate and attempt to deposit an indelible inaccurate impression and influence on your present?

Are you reaping what you have been sowing over an extended time frame? Determine to cultivate new mindsets, heading in a direction with purpose and passion. Know that God is with you. He is for you and He is working through you.

SCRIPTURE:
Isaiah 43:1-2 ESV
1"Fear not, for I have redeemed you; I have called you by name, you are mine. 2.When you pass through the waters, I will be with you; and through the rivers, they shall not overwhelm you; when you walk through fire you shall not be burned, and the flame shall not consume you."

DISTINCT DIRECTION

Distinct direction occurs when you have made up your mind that talking about change is not enough, instead, you purposefully choose to move into a new chapter of your life and do what it takes to fulfil your God-given destiny. When you possess clarity and distinct direction, that is when distractions are denied entry, which represents standing up on the inside, in Christ Jesus.

And when you recognise and function in your True Identity, in Christ, opposing forces coming against you become ineffective. As it is written in God's Word, But you belong to God, my dear children. You have already won a victory over those people, because the Spirit who lives in you is greater than the spirit who lives in the world, 1 John 4:4 NLT.

Recently, on a photo shoot, I was standing on a rock ledge, the incoming tide was impressive as the water crashed against the rocks. At times the spray would rise to a great height. I was in my element. God protected me from the effects of the waves. I was reminded of God's power at work in my life, overcoming obstacles, and walking free from the bondage associated with my past.

Be at peace, stop trying to figure things out. Resist striving and being stressed, instead lean on God's understanding and not on what you think is right in going forward. Be encouraged. You were created for a time such as this.

SCRIPTURE:
Hebrews 4:16 NLT
So let us come boldly to the throne of our gracious God. There we will receive his mercy, and we will find grace to help us when we need it most.

SING A NEW SONG

Sing a new song. Your thoughts today will become the reality of your tomorrow. What you speak is what becomes foundational in your life. What you say is what you believe in regarding your situation or circumstances.

Are you believing in God for a miracle? Or are you sweating it out, trying to work a plan where there is no solution in the natural? But with God all things are possible, only believe.

Carrying burdens and thinking you can reach your destination without consequences of exhaustion is something you need to think about carefully.

When you surrender your will to God's will, He will work through your situation and heal you of what has been distracting you for some time and attempting to dismantle your peace.

This is the time to take authority, start speaking and declaring God's Word over your situation. His Word is a Holy Prescription for whatever your need is. As with medicine, God's Word, His Bible, needs to be read, studied, meditated on, and believed daily. Always.

Flood your soul and spirit with God's Word. Drench yourself in His promises. When you do that with absolute belief and trust, the lies and deception of Satan, which have attempted to flood and drown you with disappointment, distractions, discouragement, depression, anxiety, and a whole host of other evil schemes and lies will come to nothing. That is when you raise a standard against the lies of the devil and walk from a place of victory, in Christ.

SING A NEW SONG

As a born-again believer, you have the resurrection power of Jesus Christ residing in you. Before Satan attempts to lure you into believing you are weak, remind him, applying God's Word, who and Whose you are.

Let the weak say they are strong. You have been silent for too long. And you have been battle-weary for a significant time. It's time to be loosed from every evil snare and to recognise early, the wiles of Satan. Ask God to equip and empower you with discernment in recognising Satan's recycled attacks. Only God can heal you.

Again, I do not worship Satan, but you need to seek God every day in every way, and to worship Him, in protecting you. I encourage you to sing a new song and to release the old mindsets, refrain from attempting to recapture the past, that represents stagnancy. Invite every new thing, including the challenges, that stimulate change and growth, to re-shape your thinking.

It is God's intentionality for you to be the change. To move in the miraculous. My attraction to water resulted in some near drownings, but God protected me. Do not permit circumstances to drown your hope in moving forward. God has also saved me from almost drowning in circumstances that were beyond my control, at times. Be at peace, with God, yourself, and with others: forgive. Forgiveness sets you free. Forgive yourself and those in your life. So, again, sing unto the Lord a new song.

SCRIPTURE:
1 Peter 1:3 NIV
Praise be to the God and Father of our Lord Jesus Christ! In his great mercy he has given us new birth into a living hope through the resurrection of Jesus Christ from the dead.

CALM AMONGST CHAOS

Peace within, influences peace without. In other words, you can enjoy peace and joy even in the most trying of circumstances.

How, you ask? By trusting God and working with Him as you are at the end of yourself. Working with God involves cooperating with Him as He advises you what to do, one step at a time. Being at the end of yourself is a good place to be.

When you have tried every trick and supposed solution, but the problem remains, that is when you know God is waiting for you to seek Him. Sometimes the situation is 'triggered' by external circumstances, whilst, on other occasions, it is your reaction to what could be an everyday situation.

I am not finger-pointing, or suggesting a form of exaggeration, but I have been there. And God is still healing me. There is no guilt attached to my words. But, when you have exhausted every avenue, it is time to surrender your will to God and to hear His still small voice.

As I have written before, responding to God's whisper, you need to be still and attentive. Take authority over chaos and complicated circumstances with God's peace. And His peace will flow through you as you learn to be still before Him.

Chaotic thoughts you are thinking, attract the chaos around you. When you are at peace, even in the direst situation, God can work behind the scenes. The battle belongs to the Lord.

CALM AMONGST CHAOS

If you feel 'flooded' with exhaustive and deadly emotions, anger, frustration, revenge, anxiety, here is a Godly Prescription from His Word for you, casting all your cares [all your anxieties, all your worries, and all your concerns, once and for all] on Him, for He cares about you [with deepest affection, and watches over you very carefully]. 1 Peter 5:7 AMP.

Tread carefully through each day, be at peace, love your neighbour as yourself. Keep life simple by not overindulging in details that don't relate to you.

Keep a distance from gossip, slander and minding other people's business. Being at peace and remaining in peace, represents having a clear conscience, in Christ, and a holy heart that beats in the rhythm of God's heartbeat.

SCRIPTURE:
Isaiah 59:19 AMPC.
So [as the result of the Messiah's intervention] they shall [reverently] fear the name of the Lord from the west, and His glory from the rising of the sun. When the enemy shall come in like a flood, the Spirit of the Lord will lift up a standard against him *and* put him to flight [for He will come like a rushing stream which the breath of the Lord drives].

REST AND RESTORATION

Do you feel burdened and exhausted from your current circumstances? Perhaps you are attempting to take matters into your own hands and not resting in God's peace.

If your attention is to repay someone for what they have done to you and not for you, revenge is not the solution. It deepens the root of bitterness and opens wounds that become infected and fester if you choose not to forgive. I know I have covered this subject before, but it's a reminder of letting go.

Beloved, don't be obsessed with taking revenge, but leave that to God's righteous justice. For the Scriptures say: "Vengeance is mine, and I will repay," says the Lord. Romans 12:19 TPT.

Keith, my husband, and I have recently experienced a 12-month season of life changing decisions. God taught us that when He closes doors, that we were to stop trying to re-open them. Once they are shut, it is God's intention to bless you, and not to punish you, as God is love. Frustration creeps in when you attempt to open doors that God has permanently sealed.

It is God's purpose to lead you to and through open doors. When you change your posture and your attitude, the doors start opening at an accelerated rate. Resist attempting to open doors which are closed for a reason. Reposition yourself and your thought processes and embrace change. Travel in a new direction, in your mind, and permit new, fresh, and healthy thoughts to become a reality. Thank God and trust Him in every situation.

REST AND RESTORATION

SCRIPTURES:

Here are some verses of Scripture for you to ponder on.

7. "And to the angel of the church in Philadelphia write: 'The words of the holy one, the true one, who has the key of David, who opens, and no one will shut, who shuts, and no one opens.' 8. "I know your works. Behold, I have set before you an open door, which no one is able to shut. I know that you have but little power, and yet you have kept my word and have not denied my name." Revelation 3:7-8 ESV.

Therefore, since the promise of entering his rest still stands, let us be careful that none of you be found to have fallen short of it. Hebrews 4:1 NIV.

Then he said to me, "This [continuous supply of oil] is the word of the Lord to Zerubbabel [prince of Judah], saying, 'Not by might, nor by power, but by My Spirit [of whom the oil is a symbol],' says the Lord of hosts. Zechariah 4:6 AMP.

"And I will compensate you for the years that the swarming locust has eaten, the creeping locust, the stripping locust, and the gnawing locust-My great army which I sent among you." Joel 2:25 AMP.

RHAPSODY

Rhapsody is described as, 'an effusively enthusiastic or an ecstatic expression of feeling.' Do not permit your circumstances to master you, or for you to become a servant to them. Energy and enthusiasm wane over time due to stress and responsibility if it is not shared in a balanced manner.

In Christ, you need to walk in authority when you recognise (early) the repetitive signs of recycled thinking and behavioural patterns. You are always going to be the one who will carry extra burdens if you neglect to assert your authority, in Christ. It is easy for some around you to delegate and not take responsibility. Either, they don't have the experience, professionally, or alternatively they are lacking in enthusiasm and accountability.

Now, that leaves you in a see-saw situation. They are on top, feeling buoyant, with less responsibility, and sometimes, in a leadership role and possess authority, whilst you are submerged with responsibilities and you're experiencing exhaustion, and possibly resentment.

If you don't become proactive early, in an acceptable manner, more responsibility will be deposited on you, with unrealistic expectations and deadlines. If the situation is left unattended, it develops to a place of overwhelm, which usually leads to resentment and eventual burn out.

But, as I have just written, if you don't speak up and become proactive early, nothing will change. Apart from the fact you will become frustrated and overused. Be responsible by speaking up and speaking out. Use your voice.

RHAPSODY

Be the person you want others to be for you. You possibly have a fear of man, I'm using a Biblical term, ask God for His wisdom and boldness to create an awareness of the load you are carrying which should be shared.

Thoughts that occupy your mind first thing in the morning determine your outcome for the day. Excuses are like crutches, discard them. Set your sights on the things above and be at peace, in Christ.

You are responsible for your joy by speaking up and being released into God's peace as you commit yourself to change. Resist drip feeding from others, disallow blame game. If injustice is prevalent, present your case with facts.

SCRIPTURE:
Zephaniah 3:15, 17 ESV
15.The Lord has taken away the judgments against you; He has cleared away your enemies. The King of Israel, the Lord is in your midst, you shall never again fear evil. 17.The Lord your God is in your midst, a mighty one who will save; he will rejoice over you with gladness; he will quiet you by his love; he will exult over you with loud singing.

JOY UNSPEAKABLE

You are oiled in the anointed oil of joy that breaks the yoke and surrenders and bows its knee to Jesus Christ. Rest your soul in the quietness of each moment, celebrate with the angels of your release from the spirit of grief, and become triumphant and victorious, in Him.

In Christ, after a night of mourning, joy comes, soaked in hope and harmony in the rhythm of God's heartbeat as He tenderly touches you with His hands. And you look full into His wonderful face, which become memorable, miraculous moments.

Flood your thoughts with the reality of heaven, instinctively knowing that all things are possible with God, only believe. This is the hour of breaking loose, that you choose to be freed, and unshackled from the spirit of grief.

Become strong, stable, and resilient, in Christ, with a resolve to never return to your past, refrain from leaning back to the times of deadly emotions and toxic thoughts which result in hopelessness.

Live from where God's joy erupts from the inner depths of your soul, drenching you with His power, whilst His joy, becomes yours, in Christ. Joy is your strength, in and through Him.

Whatever and whoever has attempted to hold you back and down, bless them, their words and 'transparent' thoughts, words unuttered, will come to no avail.

JOY UNSPEAKABLE

God's Word says, "I will give you the keys of the kingdom of heaven; whatever you bind on earth will be bound in heaven, and whatever you loose on earth will be loosed in heaven." Mathew 16:19 NIV.

There is no time to waste on the years that have slipped by, instead, an attitude of joy looks forward to a brighter beautiful tomorrow and a hopeful future.

Joy lightens the weight and burdens you have been carrying, as it encourages you to cast your cares upon God. Cast all your anxiety on him because he cares for you, 1 Peter 5:7 NIV.

SCRIPTURE:
Habakkuk 3:17-18 NIV
17.Though the fig tree does not bud and there are no grapes on the vines, though the olive crop fails and the fields produce no food, though there are no sheep in the pen and no cattle in the stalls, 18.yet I will rejoice in the Lord, I will be joyful in God my Savior.

SLIPSTREAMING THROUGH THIS DAY

Ship shape, slipstreaming into the brilliance of this day, floating and no flotsam, buoyant and like jetsam, discarding the poison associated with your past.

Allow every cell in your body to tingle with electricity and excitement in and through God's Spirit. Expect good things to happen today. What you perceive, you receive, whether positive or negative.

You are born to be free. Some of you could be like an over tightened musical instrument, intense, and on the brink of bursting with sustained stress.

Lighten up, lessen your load, be balanced. What you carry today, will be inherited tomorrow. Be carriers of God's greatness. Celebrate yourself, your DNA, you are fearfully and wonderfully made, in Christ.

Separate the Truth of God and his Word, from the lies of Satan, and live in the Light and Truth of Jesus Christ. Which voice are you listening to, the one from the balcony or the one from the bunker?

Unwind, soak in the stillness of intended serenity. Do the same things differently. Stop repeating the same old thing, expecting new results. Change is vital, firstly, in you and in your circumstances. In Christ, you are the change.

SLIPSTREAMING THROUGH THIS DAY

Speak well of yourself, everything originates from within, develop inner strength, by reading what God says about you in His Word. In Christ you are free and captivating, and not captured or confined.

In Christ, you are a victor, not a victim. Ease effectively into the wonder of every minute, leave your mark on this day, with your fingerprint of uniqueness - softly, subtly and with quiet determination. That's the way.

This is no ordinary day, in Christ, it is as extraordinary and as exceptional as you are, choose to live above your circumstances as you are seated in heavenly places with Jesus.

2."Enlarge the site of your tent [to make room for more children]; stretch out the curtains of your dwellings, do not spare them; lengthen your tent ropes and make your pegs (stakes) firm [in the ground]. 3.For you will spread out to the right and to the left; and your descendants will take possession of nations and will inhabit deserted cities." Isaiah 54:2, 3 AMP.

SCRIPTURE:
Psalm 4:8 NLT
In peace I will lie down and sleep, for you alone, O Lord, will keep me safe.

NEVER GIVE UP

Dream and believe that you are on the brink of breakthrough, you are preparing to walk into your destiny. Speak it, see it, and occupy its reality. Sow seeds of abundance to be a blessing to others.

Spend time with your loved ones and your children. One cannot buy back time. Quality time is not simply a sacrifice, it is an essential ingredient. Going forward, passing the baton, what a legacy you will leave for future generations.

Listen, love, laugh. You are no second fiddle, but you're an instrument of integrity and influence. You need to believe you are not a failure if something didn't work out.

Sometimes it's seeing life from a different perspective, with persistence, dogged determination, and endurance, and equipped with God's grace, which will reward you with fulfilment. Some of the world's greatest leaders and scientists, failed on numerous occasions before they were successful.

Be the best you, in Christ, the best in what you do, but do not compete, instead complete each other. Be good to yourself. Everything manifested without originates from within.

Be quietly confident and humble, developing character. Humility breeds greatness, live in the Light and Truth of Christ, and come out from the shadows.

NEVER GIVE UP

Develop the child in you, life is lived at an accelerated rate. Learn to embrace life and to trust God, like a child. Especially today, as life is highly technical, sophisticated, and often complicated. Children attract the good things in life, and they believe in the best. And so should you.

Stand in awe and wonder of miraculous moments. Leaning and posturing into the present, which is a gift for the future. Learn what life is teaching you. Above all else, share and care. Have an inspirational day.

When you persevere with dogged determination and faith in God, you will cross the finish line and your life will be an influence on others around you who are stuck.

SCRIPTURE:
Hebrews 13:5 AMP
"Let your character [your moral essence, your inner nature] be free from the love of money [shun greed-be financially ethical], being content with what you have; for He has said, "I will never [under any circumstances] desert you [nor give you up nor leave you without support, nor will I in any degree leave you helpless], nor will I forsake or let you down or relax My hold on you [assuredly not]!"

BE PREPARED FOR A MIRACLE

Preparation is paramount. It is directional and intentional. It prevents overwhelm. If you're unprepared, you're potentially vulnerable regarding what lies ahead.

Go where you have never been before, in the goodness of God. Explore new territories. Never give up. Stop swirling to other people's expectancy of you. Life is precious. Take time to smell the roses and to count your blessings.

Look forward, plan ahead. Step into something you're unfamiliar with. Keep advancing with steady footsteps. Live a life that is bigger than you could ever imagine. God's timing is perfect.

I heard God speak to my heart to encourage those who have been experiencing, what seems like endless storms. Breakthrough is coming. God is the Anchor of your soul. Be still and know that I am God. Psalm 46:10. Be encouraged.

Be led by your instincts and not by your feelings. Achievement is accomplished through active faith. Be expectant for what God has already prepared for you. Live in hope. Something good is about to happen to you.

SCRIPTURE:
Psalm 77:14 NIV
You are the God who performs miracles; you display your power among the peoples.

THINKING OF YOU ON MOTHER'S DAY

This Mother's Day, from my heart to yours, whoever you are, wherever you are, I'm reaching out to you with a heart that is for you and with you.

Whether you have experienced acute sadness either through a miscarriage(s), a stillborn, and to you who have lost a child or children through an illness or an accident, and also to those of you who are 'journeying' through IV, God is with you.

It is also a time of remembering those of you who have lost your mother, I honour you, please know that my heart is with you.

Mother's Day is not altogether sad and associated with pain and grief, but for many it is a day of discomfort, anguish, struggle, mixed emotions, and memories.

This Mother's Day, I wish you comfort, God's love, and peace for those of you who are suffering, and hope and expectancy from this moment forward.

Be sensitive to those who are unable to celebrate this day, as a result of loss. Shalom.

SCRIPTURE:
Isaiah 66:13 ESV
As one whom his mother comforts, so I will comfort you; you shall be comforted in Jerusalem.